MW00355381

Life in the FAT Lane

A Memoir

Lisa D'Elena-Borges

Life in the Fat Lane

Copyright © 2020 Lisa D'Elena Borges.

Produced and printed
by Stillwater River Publications.
All rights reserved. Written and produced in the
United States of America. This book may not be reproduced
or sold in any form without the expressed, written
permission of the author and publisher.

Visit our website at
www.StillwaterPress.com
for more information.

First Stillwater River Publications Edition

ISBN: 978-1-952521-13-3

1 2 3 4 5 6 7 8 9 10
Written by Lisa D'Elena Borges
Published by Stillwater River Publications,
Pawtucket, RI, USA.

The views and opinions expressed
in this book are solely those of the author
and do not necessarily reflect the views
and opinions of the publisher.

*This book is dedicated to everyone who has had
or is currently facing a personal struggle.
Remember, you are not alone.*

CONTENTS

INTRODUCTION

I haven't always been fat. In fact, I used to be very thin. There was a time in my life when I was too thin; however, it was attributed to the environment I grew up in and not a personal choice. People also said I was pretty. I've never had much self-confidence; so looking back at pictures, I guess maybe I was pretty. I'm just not one of those girls who walk around knowing that I am beautiful, I'm not sure I'll ever see myself that way. To me being pretty and being thin go hand in hand. It just seems natural that it would, especially since we live in a celebrity crazed world where there is so much focus on beauty and size. Unfortunately, Hollywood seems to set the standard for the rest of us. It is only recently that there is an acceptance of plus size models and a small handful of plus size actresses in Hollywood, although I recently read an article online about singer Bebe Rexha not being able to find a designer to dress her for the red carpet at the Grammys. According to what I read, she's a size 8! Designers actually consider her "too big." That is a shame. To me being a size 8 would be a dream come true.

As I sit here and begin to write this book, I can tell you that I don't feel very pretty and I certainly am not thin. In fact, I'm far from being thin. I dream about the day that I am thin again. In all honesty I don't know any more what my thin will be. I have to be realistic; I'll never be a size 7 again.

So, what happened over the course of time that I went from what people called "too thin" to finding myself sitting here writing a book about being fat? There's the very simple answer: I OVEREAT and I don't exercise. That's it in a nutshell, right? Wrong. The reality is that in my case it's much more complex than simply overeating. Every person has a unique story to tell, and I'm here to tell you about my own personal story.

I can tell you that I have many emotional issues from the past and I have learned that I must come to terms with those issues or I will never be able to move forward. My weight issues stem from more than just overeating; it's so much more complicated than that. It's not just one reason but many reasons mixed together. Combine those that I've come to realize: emotional issues and ghosts from the past; my love for cooking; (and eating, of course, c'mon who doesn't like to eat?) my dislike of exercising (it's just so boring); emotional eating whether I'm stressed, sad, mad, or even the mere fact that I'm bored. It could be work related, relationship related, bad childhood memories, low self-esteem, or no self-worth among many other things. My overeating could be triggered by one of those elements or by any combination. So just to summarize, my weight issues are a combination of many factors, not merely that I overeat, and that is why I believe it is far more difficult for me to lose weight than it may first appear.

Anyone who is in my position can find an excuse to eat and we don't have to look very hard for those excuses either. It doesn't always have to be a negative trigger that causes overeating and binging. Happy celebratory moments contribute as well: birthdays, holidays, promotions, weddings, oh the celebration list is long. You get so used to overeating that you just don't know when to stop.

I've finally reached the point where I am done! I'm done with being fat, (it sure has taken me long enough to get to this point) I'm taking my life back. I'm determined to take my life back while I'm still young enough to enjoy it and do something worthwhile with it. While I take my life back, I invite you to come along on my journey and I hope that along the way I can make you laugh and maybe even inspire you. If you are reading this and are not a person of size, I hope that I can help you to realize what it's like for those who struggle with their weight.

What you need to remember is that this book is being written by a "real" person. An average, everyday ordinary person like you, not a celebrity or wealthy person who can write a check to hire a personal trainer, a personal chef, or nannies to watch their kids so they can have hours at the gym and focus on themselves. I am just the girl next door, someone who works two jobs, has two kids, and leads a super active life. I am a person just like you who worries about paying bills, about what to cook for dinner, and how to get two kids to two different places at the same time. I deal with everyday issues and the stress of daily living. I spread myself too thin at times and occasionally overbook myself. I've been inspired to make a change for the better in all aspects of my life and that's just what I'm going to do.

I am not going to sit here and pretend that I'm a fitness guru, or a nutrition expert. I am not, nor will I ever be. I don't pretend that when this journey is over that you will see me come out with the latest greatest workout video. This is not a diet program. This is a story about my life and the struggles of being overweight. This is real life for me and for so many other people who are overweight. I'm going to tell it like it is about being fat, about the challenges that people like me have to face every day. I'm not a doctor or expert in anything to do with dieting (unless you want to call me an expert in failing at diets). What I am an expert on is living life as a larger person, an expert on struggling with my weight, and an expert on doing everything the hard way.

I just want to tell my story and talk about life the way I see it. I will talk about things that people don't think about when they are sitting there judging us for the way we look and not appreciating what we have to offer the world. Others can judge us, but they have no idea why we are fat. They don't think about the fact that some people have medical issues that prevent them from losing weight, or how some may have deep rooted issues from childhood and turn to food for comfort and simply don't know how to stop eating.

While writing this book about being of a larger size, I've begun a new journey of my own. I've started dieting and exercising and changing my life. They say that you will lose weight when you are ready, you can't do it for anyone else but yourself. This is true. I've been up and down with my weight for so many years, tried all kinds of diets, would try to lose weight to be in a friend's wedding or some other event, then finally one day I decided to just do it for me and be done with this battle. I want to change direction. I've been traveling in the fat lane for too long, I'm taking a turn onto the road to thin. I'd like to share that journey with you as well.

Come along whether you agree with the things I have to say or not. I promise it will be an interesting ride.

Traveling in the FAT Lane

COMING CLEAN

You know as well as I do that it's never polite to ask a woman her weight or her age, but you didn't ask did you (I know that's what you are thinking though... how much does/did she weigh?)? Let's address this right off the bat. Let's just get it out of the way because we all know that this is the elephant in the room. I'll come clean, total transparency.

They say that the first step to recovery or fixing a problem is admitting you have a problem, so here I am admitting I have a problem. I have a problem that I should have addressed long ago. Why I didn't get a handle on this when it was a smaller issue, I can't say for sure. I guess I just wasn't ready. I certainly did not ever think that my weight issues would escalate to the point they are at today. I never envisioned myself to be morbidly obese. I do know that I need to do a lot of self-examination and make a lot of changes in my life. As I promised I'm going to come clean with you (and the world) and admit how much I weigh. It's very upsetting and very embarrassing to me that I have let myself get to this point. It's very disconcerting that I did not think enough of myself in the past to do something about my weight gain before it got out of control. You would think that once I started to gain weight, I would have said to myself, "Hey Lisa, you've gained ten pounds, go out and exercise and cut back on what you're eating," but I didn't. Nope, I always have to do everything the hard way.

That is all in the past now isn't it? The next line I'm going to write is very difficult (I've been trying to find a way to avoid writing this, but I can't, it must be done). I am going to write it and I never want to see or read it again. Once this chapter is complete, I never want to look back at it and I certainly never, ever want to live through this or weigh this again.

As of today (today being the day I decided to write this book) I weigh three hundred pounds. There, I said it. It's out there for the whole world to see. Now anyone who knows me well knows that it takes a lot to embarrass me. I can talk about anything. I can be the biggest jokester and do the silliest of things and not be embarrassed, but admitting how much weight I gained is one thing that does embarrass me. In fact, it makes me feel more than embarrassed. I look at that number and I look at myself in the mirror and I want to crawl under a rock and die. It is something that is so painful to me.

Does it make me feel better to write that down and come clean? Not really. Writing that one sentence has literally brought me to tears. It literally pains my heart to know that I let myself get to that point. I can't stop asking myself, how did I let this happen, and why did I live like this for so long? Why did I just accept my fatness? Why was that okay when I am such a fighter? I will fight for a cause I believe in until I win. I don't give up when it's something important to me; I find a way to make things happen. One of the biggest compliments I ever got was when my boss said I was tenacious. I will move mountains to make things happen. I guess for some reason my weight gain must not have been important to me. I guess maybe it was the fact that *I* was not important to me.

With every pound I gained I swore I would never let myself get to the 300-pound mark. I started getting concerned at 150, then 175, then 200. Once I hit 250, I vowed that I would lose weight and I would never, ever hit 300 pounds. However, once I crept up to that 300-pound mark, I completely stopped caring. I didn't even tell myself that I wouldn't hit it, I just remember saying one day, "I guess it's going to happen, so be it." Once I said that to myself, I didn't care anymore about anything I ate. I just ate whatever I wanted, whenever I wanted.

So, what happened? Many things happened. I got caught up with life, maybe I stopped caring—well let's be honest, it's not maybe I stopped caring, I DID stop. Had I cared enough about myself I would have never gotten to such a big number on the scale. Had I cared about myself at all, I would have wanted to lose weight when I gained the first ten pounds. I let my low self-esteem take control of my life. I didn't realize my worth. I was too lazy to take control and do something about it. Not to mention that the more weight I gained the more daunting the task of dieting seemed.

I could go on and on with reasons and excuses but that is not going to do me any good, I need to move forward. All of that is in the past now. It's a new day and I've made a conscious decision to lose this weight once and for all. I am throwing away all the excuses, I'm putting my big girl pants on and I'm going to own it. It's nobody else's fault that I gained so much weight and it's nobody else's decision to lose this weight. It's time to take responsibility for that. It's time to take control!

I also need to be very thankful that during the many years of weight gain I did not develop any medical issues. In fact, when I stop and think about some of the problems that could have occurred, and the fact that it would have been my own fault and totally preventable as well, all I can say is that I'm pretty darn lucky.

Forgiveness is another key word to focus on here. I need to forgive myself. Forgiving is part of the healing process. Yes, I failed myself in many areas. Some things in my life that led me to the fat lane were not my fault; however, letting those things take control of my life is my fault. My mom used to tell me that life is about starting over; every time I got into trouble she'd say let's start over, tomorrow is a new day. Well, those words ring true today. It's time to start over and that is just what I'm going to do.

So, coming clean did not make me feel good at all, but it had to be done. I had to put it out there and face the demon(s) that have haunted me for many years. Now that I have done it and made the decision to reverse that number on the scale and take my life back, I feel much better. I feel like I can finally move forward with my life.

SUPPORT

One thing that I have learned rather quickly is that a support system is key, even if there is only one person that you can count on. No matter who you are or where you come from, you can find a friend or family member who is going to be your champion through thick and thin. We all have at least one person in our lives that we can count on and trust completely. We all have at least one person that will be there no matter what and will want to walk by your side on this journey. If you have more than one person, well, you are somebody truly special, because it's been my experience that if you can find one person that is there for you no matter what then you are lucky.

It is so important to have someone in your life who will encourage and challenge you. To find that person all you need to do is look around your circle of family and friends, pick one, and ask them for help. People like to feel needed, especially if they know it's for something so important to you. I know for me and so many others asking is the hardest part. We hate to ask for anything, we want to do everything by ourselves and not burden anyone, but what we don't realize is our true friends will be there for us. All we've got to do is say the word. Think about it, if someone came to you and asked you for help, wouldn't you help if you could? Of course you would. There have been many studies on human nature that show people like to feel trusted and needed by others. You have to do the hard work, but you don't have to be alone while doing it.

If you are inspired to lose the fat once and for all, pick that one person that you absolutely trust and come clean. Lay it all out there. Tell him or her what your goals are, where you've been, and where you want to go. If that is too much for you to openly say (and after writing my weight down and seeing it on paper, I know how difficult it is to say out loud; in fact to this day I have not said that number out loud) then write it on a piece of paper. Write your goals and write down your starting weight, stick it in an envelope and seal it, give it to that person that you chose and ask them to hold it in a safe place. When you feel comfortable you can open it together and celebrate your accomplishments.

Just remember this: when you write down that number that is on the scale, that will be the last time you ever see that number again. It's all downhill from there.

I believe that by writing down what you weigh on that piece of paper, or by telling your confidante your weight in complete honesty, you are releasing it, getting a "weight" off your shoulders. You don't have to tell the whole world, but I'm willing to bet you that once you complete your journey you will want to tell everyone because you'll be so proud of your accomplishment and how hard you worked to reach your weight goals.

When I decided to begin this journey, I made a personal decision to make it very public. By doing it this way, I gave myself no room for failure. I started a blog where I could write my thoughts, failures, and successes. I shared that blog on social networks, and I had my person, my cheer-leader. Little did I know by making this journey public I would end up with a whole support team. I jokingly refer to them as "Team Lisa," but having this support team truly makes all the difference in the world for me. I am the one who has to do the work by making daily decisions on what to eat and find exercises I can do and live with, but knowing that I have a team of people behind me, a team rooting me on, and a team who will listen with a sympathetic ear and then give me a kick in the butt to jumpstart my motivation again really makes a difference on this journey.

I know not everyone wants to come clean in public but my point is that if you are beginning a weight loss journey of your own, the support will be there for you, and having your own "team of cheerleaders" on standby will make the journey so much easier and so much more fun than going it alone. Trust me, you will be amazed to see who will be standing in your corner for you.

SETTING GOALS AND REWARDS

Everyone has different motivators. I am the type of person who absolutely needs motivators. They keep me going and give me something to look forward to. I need to have short-term goals and long-term goals. That is what works for me, but what works for me may not work for you. Just like our fingerprints are unique to us so are the reasons we gain and lose weight. There is nobody in this world that knows you like you know yourself.

I have spent much time thinking about the goals that I want to achieve and how I'm going to get there and what is going to keep me motivated and moving forward.

This is what I've come up with for my long-term goals:
- I will lose a minimum of 100 pounds. I say a minimum because once I've reached that goal, I will evaluate how I look and how I feel and if I think I have more to lose or want to lose, I'm going to go for it. I just can't make that determination until I've reached my minimum goal.
- I will celebrate my 100-pound weight loss with a trip; preferably a cruise.

My short-term goals:

- Every 10 pounds I will celebrate with a fun movie night out with friends.
- Every 50 pounds I will get a tattoo. This means I will have a minimum of two tattoos.

My reasoning for these goals and rewards are simple. I will reward myself for my successes with things that I love. When I've dieted in the past, I rewarded myself with food, very ironic. This time is different; food is no longer used for a reward. One hundred pounds is a big goal to reach (think about what one hundred boxes of butter looks like) so for this goal I need something huge (no pun intended). There are few things I love more than travel, so it seems appropriate for me to take a trip to celebrate this success.

That takes care of my long-term goal. I get bored very easily; it's very hard for me to stay focused so I need to have mini goals. I did not want to reward myself with new clothes because obviously losing weight you need to get new clothes. I don't believe in "rewarding" myself with a "necessity." I have a love affair with movies, so I think ten pounds is a reasonable amount to reach to have an evening out with friends and see a movie.

Why a tattoo you ask? Well, part of this journey for me is to face my fears, to do what I always perceived to be the unthinkable and to meet new challenges head on. I've always wanted a tattoo and have always been petrified of how painful it might be. However, by writing this book is I am facing things in my past that were very painful, as well as facing the pain of being fat for all those years. Therefore it only seems fitting that I get past all the pain and fear and face and conquer the unknown pain of getting a tattoo. These are my basic goals, something to keep me motivated and help me stay on track.

There are people out there who may not need as many motivators as I do or any at all for that matter. Everyone is different; there is no right or wrong, it's just what works for you.

NO ESCAPE

Let's face it, overeating is an addiction but unlike a drug, drinking, or gambling addiction, there is no escape from food. It seems to me that alcoholics and drug addicts and even gamblers get more empathy than overeaters. Where is the empathy for the fat people? We also have issues that drive us to overeat just like those that have issues that drive them to drink, abuse drugs, and gamble. I believe that in some cases people overeat for the same reasons that some people will use drugs, drink alcohol, and spend their hard earned money at the casino.

There are warnings everywhere for the aforementioned addictions; for example, you go to the casino and there are phone numbers for Gamblers Anonymous on every slot machine and the doors to the building. Everywhere you turn you can find advertisements and messages about drinking responsibly—hell you go on a cruise and they have AA meetings. I think they should have overeating meetings on the cruise as well. You can go to rehab for substance abuse and drinking problems, you can go to Gamblers Anonymous... you can learn to live without your drug or alcohol of choice, but you can't live without food. We all know that we need food to survive, so in my eyes a food addiction is a bit harder to overcome. This is not to take away from the severity or difficulty of other addictions. I'm just saying that I know you can live without the drugs and alcohol just like you can live by never stepping foot in a casino again, I've seen people succeed. If you stop eating, you die.

Think about it; if you're an alcoholic and finally decided to get help, you've gone through your twelve-step program, you've been sober for years, and you get invited to a dinner party. I know it must be a struggle to be there watching everyone around you drink while you've got a diet cola in your hand, but you make it through and you can go home proud of yourself. Now imagine that you have an eating addiction and you're invited to a dinner party; well guess what, you are there to eat dinner right? You can't pass on food; what you can do is learn how to be in control of what you are eating, because you can't just never eat again. So, while I have the greatest respect for anyone who has taken control of an addiction, I believe that a food addiction is just as hard if not harder to conquer.

Sure, there are all kinds of diet programs, pills, and surgeries available to us; there is even an Overeaters Anonymous with its own twelve-step program. Alcoholics can live long happy lives once they become clean and sober, they can learn how to handle themselves in social environments without a drink. As difficult as it may be it can be done. I have many friends who have done just that. I would say that overeaters have a more difficult time as they are consistently put into environments where food is the focus; you are hard pressed to find an environment that is food free.

Bad day at work, let's go for ice cream. Something wonderful happens in your life, let's go to dinner to celebrate. Birthdays, christenings, bar mitzvahs, communions, holidays; you name it, there's food. It seems like food is the centerpiece for any occasion. We lose focus of the event and the fact that we will be surrounded by friends and family, some of whom we don't see that often.

We have this need to impress with food. Especially if you come from an Italian family like mine where, god forbid, the party ends, and you don't have a week's worth of leftovers. The more leftovers you have the better the party. The more food the better, the more impressive the food, the more successful the event. We need to have appetizers and main dishes and desserts... yes, the desserts, the best part of any party especially when there is a dessert buffet involved. Not only do we need to have a cake, but we must have a dessert table, we must have choices.

I've been hosting Christmas Eve at my house for over twenty-five years and every year my husband would say the same thing: "Why did you get so many desserts?" My reply: "People like choices." Let's be serious, if you are expecting a houseful of something like twenty to thirty people, are you really going to offer one dessert? I think not. For some reason it bothers him that I have more than one dessert, but maybe he's on to something. I say, have you ever gone to a party and not had a choice of dessert? I can see if you have a small group of people over for dinner, well of course you have one dessert, but at a party, I don't think that's overkill. But I digress... the point is that it is just in my blood to have options and that just shows how obsessed I have become with food.

Not only do I supply the bulk of the food for any given holiday or party, but guests will call to respond to the invite and say what can I bring, because you should never go anywhere empty handed, that's just proper etiquette right? Etiquette is especially important in an Italian family. If you show up empty handed you can guarantee you'll be talked about for months to come. Italians don't forget. In fact, you'll be talked about until the next party when someone else shows up empty handed and takes the crown from you.

So, now I have all the food that was on my menu plus all the food brought by guests. People will come and be excitedly overwhelmed by so much food and so many choices. The hostess will beam with pride as she overhears a guest share the story of how much food was at the party. When in reality what I really should do is make a menu and when my guests call to ask what they can bring I should give them a choice from what was already planned. Why don't I do that? Well, I'll tell you why: it's because I wonder, what if we just don't have enough? What if they bring the wrong kind? What if they promised to bring the dish and then something happened so they could not make it to the party (that's happened before). Or worse... what if they are a terrible cook (but think that they are the greatest cook in the world), and they don't have enough sense to bring a store bought item? I just obsess so much over the quantity and quality of food. There is just too much focus on the food. Somehow, I have got to learn to enjoy the actual event rather than focus on the food.

Occasionally I will host a potluck dinner; this means that myself and everyone invited will provide their favorite dish, a dish meaning one item. This way the hostess does not have to provide the bulk of the food nor bear the bulk of the cost for the party, sounds good right? Should be a simple concept to grasp. Apparently, I do not get the meaning of potluck, even if it is my own party. What do I do? I provide three or four of my favorite dishes. God forbid we don't have enough food. It must be how I was brought up—a fear of not having enough has been instilled in this brain and it's hard to overcome that.

So, let's be honest... repeat after me... I LIKE TO EAT. It's true; I'm not going to lie about it. I love to eat; it's an enjoyable experience. Whether you like the creamy taste of ice cream or the crunchiness of a potato chip or a big huge bowl of pasta, we look forward to eating. We look forward to holiday gatherings and the potluck parties. It's not just sweets that we enjoy and overindulge in. I have friends that don't like sweets so much, but they love their pasta. I have known people who cook a whole roast in the dead of night and sit there and eat the entire thing.

It doesn't matter if it's from the four food groups or if it's the junk; it's in our lives every day to stay. We need to learn to handle it correctly. We need to not let food control us, we need to control the food.

We all know that a big part of losing weight is portion control, so why is it so hard to control your portions and why is it so hard to stop eating? We love going to restaurants where you leave with three days of leftovers. Why do we want to go to those fancy restaurants where you leave hungry because there was not enough on your plate? Maybe that's where I should start going. Maybe that's how to control the portions when eating out.

I can't speak for anyone but myself, and for myself. I can say sometimes it's because it tastes good and I just can't get enough. Sometimes it's for comfort while other times it's because I experienced food insecurities as a child and part of my brain tells me to get it all now because I don't know when I can eat again. Then there are the times when I'm having a bad day and I'll have a big ol' chocolate bar or a pint of ice cream and it's just like getting a great big hug from your best friend. So, as I said before, my relationship with food is very complex for many different reasons.

The difference is when you get that hug from your best friend it doesn't leave you with an extra pound or two. You can get that hug from your friend and go home. When you are home getting that hug from the ice cream, well, it doesn't leave you quite as satisfied. Instead you find yourself still searching for something else once you've finished that pint.

STARVING KIDS IN AFRICA SYNDROME

Why is it so hard to stop eating? Ok, besides the obvious that it tastes so good, I'd like to take this moment to blame all the people who've told you to finish what's on your plate because there are starving kids in Africa who would love to have the food that is on your plate. So, even though you were not hungry, you were forced to finish every bite. You were guilted into it. It has become a habit that when a plate is put in front of you, you are expected to finish every bite whether you like it or not, or whether you are hungry or not.

Seriously... if I don't finish what is on my plate what am I supposed to do... put it in a Tupperware container and ship it to Africa? I'm sure by the time it got there even the African kids wouldn't want to eat it.

It's okay not to finish what's on your plate. It's okay to have leftovers. It's okay to eat half of your meal and save the other half for the next day. It's even okay if you don't like something. If you don't like it don't eat it. Why would you force yourself to eat calories that you don't enjoy? If I'm going to eat something you better believe I'm going to enjoy it. In fact, it now makes me happy to leave something behind.

One day I bought a cookie while at the mall. I took one bite of it and I didn't care for it. My normal reaction would be to just finish it anyway, after all there are starving kids in Africa who would kill for that cookie. As I thought about this, I decided to toss that cookie in the trash. I just heard you gasp... yes, I did. I tossed that cookie in the trash because I didn't like it and if I'm going to eat those calories, I want it to be worth it and enjoy it. So, to all the starving kids in Africa, I'm sorry I didn't eat that cookie but I would do it again if it meant forcing myself to eat something I didn't really want.

To current and future parents, don't tell your kids to finish what's on their plate because of the starving kids in Africa. By the time they figure out what that really means they will have created a habit of eating what they really don't want.

THE NO DESSERT CLAUSE

I am sure that every person reading this has been told at one time or another to finish what's on their plate or they will get no dessert. This is what I call the No Dessert Clause. It's part of the mealtime contract. This clause is announced at the beginning of the meal. You agree to this contract the moment you take your first bite.

Parents dangle this No Dessert Clause over a child's head to try to get them to eat more, or to eat their vegetables, and it becomes a habit. The habit being eating everything on your plate whether you are hungry or not, whether you like what's on your plate or not. I don't know about you, but if I have something on my plate I don't like, why would I want to waste calories eating that item? As understandable as it is to try to get children to eat vegetables or other foods that they don't like, it seems silly to me to use dessert as bribery, especially when this becomes a daily routine. It seems to me that dessert should not be a course served daily. It should be something special, perhaps once or twice a week, or perhaps only on weekends.

The No Dessert Clause is clearly a bribe, and parents should spend a little more time and effort into thinking about better foods to offer rather than depending on the threat of no dessert to help them out.

When you dine out, your server always asks if you saved room for dessert even as they are taking away your plate that clearly you haven't finished because you were too full. To them, it's just an upsell for a bigger tip. Now, wouldn't it be funny when dining at a restaurant if your server said to you, "If you don't eat everything on your plate, I won't be asking you if you want dessert."

THE GRANDMOTHER SYNDROME

We all have been there... the Sunday visit to grandma's house. Yes, you walk in and greet her with a hug and a kiss and the first words out of her mouth... "Are you hungry dear?" Or how about this one: "You're getting too skinny, you need to eat." Yes, those loveable grannies, no matter what your heritage, the second you walk into their house they want to feed you.

It's no use telling them you are not hungry, they will force feed you. They will pull cold chicken out of the refrigerator and ask you if you want it heated up. They will offer you the Three C's: cake and cookies and candy. Then they will stand over you smiling as they watch you eat every bite.

It doesn't matter what time of day you visit, there will be food shoved down your throat whether you want it or not.

This is not limited to their house either. When they come visit you at your home, you can bet that in that huge bag they carry there's a sandwich of some sort or a sweet treat that they brought just for you.

I remember one time going on a road trip, it was my dad and my grandmother and myself. We were traveling from Cranston, Rhode Island to Atlantic City, New Jersey. We were looking at about a six hour drive. We left early in the morning; it may have been about 6:00 a.m. As soon as we hit the highway, Grandma reached into her bag and pulled out an egg salad sandwich and asked if anybody wanted one. You would have thought we were back in the frontier days with the food supply she brought along.

This led to my own bad habits where every time I went on a road trip I needed to pack snacks, and not healthy snacks either, but what I liked to refer to as fun food: candy, chips, etc. Food that you don't normally eat, but because you're on vacation it's ok to binge.

Snacks are ok to have, but just because you are taking a little vacation it's really no excuse to go on a binge. It's just another sneaky way we convince ourselves that it's ok to eat as much as we want. We tell ourselves there's no calories in the food that we eat on vacation.

EAT IT TIL IT'S EVEN

Have you ever opened up the freezer and grabbed that container of ice cream thinking, "I'll just have a few spoonfuls." You grab your spoon and the ice cream, stand over the counter eating right out of the container. After a few spoonfuls you say, "I'm just going to eat it until it's even."

The trouble is it's never even until you've reached an empty container.

Enough Said.

SHOPPING

It has to be the number one worst thing that oversized people have to do: CLOTHES SHOPPING.

I hate it. You are limited in the number of stores that you can go to because not every store has a plus size section. Some of the stores that do have plus size sections hold you hostage to bad fashion.

You look at something on the rack and it looks sort of cute and you go try it on in the dressing room and you look like a walking disaster. You might as well just go to the tent store, you might have better luck.

Half the time I don't want to even try anything on in the dressing room—do I really want to look at myself in those full-length mirrors, or even worse, the open 360 degree mirrors? No thank you, just a reminder of how much weight I have to lose and how long it's going to take me. I take it home only to find out it doesn't fit right or look right and then I have to go back to the store, so not only is my self-esteem shot to hell, but I've wasted my time.

I envy the skinny girls that can walk into a "regular" store and go to the clearance rack and pick anything and it will look good on them. Let's face facts: it's expensive to be fat. The clothes are expensive; if you find a good sale the store never has your size. They usually have the smaller sizes available. And why are there "small" sizes in a plus size store; they have their own stores why do they have to infiltrate ours? Fat clothes are always more expensive than the "skinny clothes." In some stores you will see a rack with all sizes on it and on top of the rack you will see a sign that reads *plus sizes two dollars more.* Well, I'll give that to them, I mean it does take more material to make a bigger size, but go to a plus size specialty store and you pay an arm and a leg.

When you do find something that looks somewhat decent you end up buying it in black because the pretty colors draw more attention to you. God forbid we draw attention to ourselves. We are usually trying to hide so nobody looks at us. Someday I want to buy something red. Red says, "Hey look at me!" Red is a powerful color, a color of self-confidence. When I do buy something red you better believe I will look good in it. I have a closet full of black—one day black will be a color of the past. Well, maybe not completely because it is stylish. Everyone needs that little black dress for a cocktail party, but you get the drift.

Then there are the tricks that you play on yourself, like the time that I found a pair of pants that I absolutely loved but they didn't have my size, they had a size bigger or a size smaller. I just had to have them so I bought the size bigger because I figured if I bought the next size up, it would make me feel like I lost weight. And of course, people did notice they were "a bit big" and "noticed that I lost weight." I had people tell me, "You look like you've lost weight." So I would just go with it and say thank you.

Sometimes that plan can backfire. Like the time I was in Disney World and put on a pair of shorts that were a bit too big. I walked around the park no problem (maybe had to lift and adjust just a bit). We had to take a bus to one of the hotel properties and as I stepped off the bus my shorts fell all the way down to the ground. My daughter said she had never seen me move so fast as I bent down and pulled them back up before the whole bus got a look. (Luckily I can laugh at myself because it was pretty funny, also luckily I had underwear on). Lesson learned! Make sure you buy the right size pants or at least wear a belt.

I really would like to know why plus size clothes look like old lady clothes. No offense to older people but I'm not old, I want to look hip and trendy. With the rising rates of obesity, you would think that the designers of the world would jump into this market. I don't know about you, but there are not many places I can shop at that are stylish and affordable for the average person. The plus size section at Target is one or two racks, (although I am happy to report that recently I was in a newly remodeled Target store and they had expanded their plus size department, including plus size mannequins) the plus size section at Walmart is just plain ugly. Fat people deserve nice pretty clothes too, why do they want to make us look worse than we already feel? Lane Bryant is just too darn expensive. Fashion Bug used to have a great plus size section but they went out of business years ago. There is Dress Barn Woman, but stores are few and far between. I have found a store called the Avenue and they do have some very cute things and are very reasonably priced, but it's a hit or miss; sometimes I find lots of things that I like and other days I find nothing. That was my store of choice. I shopped there for years until it recently closed. They had great sales. Avenue online is still a thing, but with clothing I like to go to the store to see what I'm getting.

Try the internet you say. Yes, you certainly can go that route, but it can be troublesome not being able to feel the material or try the item on when it arrives, and if it doesn't fit you have to pack it all up and ship it back. Case and point, I recently made a purchase from a website called RoseGal. They have the cutest clothes. I bit the bullet and ordered a top and some leggings. They shipped fast enough, but when I tried them on they didn't fit right. There was no packing slip in the box so I had to call the company. They offered for me to keep the merchandise and get twenty percent refunded, or I could return it for a different item, or I could return it for a refund, but it was a difficult process. You have to wait for a return slip, then you have to pay the shipping fees. So, unless you are sure of the brand and your size, internet shopping may not be practical.

The other thing that ticks me off about shopping in general—and we are not talking about clothes shopping, but shopping for other items—is that when you walk into a store, particularly a boutique type of store, the sales clerk doesn't give you the time of day. (Like on *Pretty Woman*, you know the scene). They have no idea who you may be shopping for or how much money is in your pocket. They don't seem to care; they give you a dirty look and move on to the skinny customer. I have experienced this behavior firsthand. I've gone into several high-end stores and have had the salesperson walk right by without acknowledging me only to see her start chatting it up with a customer who walked in behind me and just so happened to be thinner than me. When this occurs, I will never step foot into that store again and I send them a letter letting them know this. Sales people need to be taught to treat every customer like they are their only customer.

I have noticed that as you lose weight and start to get brave enough to shop, you just can't find anything that you like. It's like when you go out and have no money, you see everything you want. When you have money, you can't find a darn thing. It's the same premise... when you are at your worst and are not looking to buy anything at all, you see lots of beautiful clothes (granted, you can't fit in them) but when your clothes start getting too big on you and you need to go out and replace them, you can't find anything you like.

While we are on the subject, let's talk stripes and pat-
terns. We've all heard the fashion rule: fat people should
never wear horizontal stripes. By the way, who sits around
and makes up these fashion rules, is there some kind of
secret committee who sits around the table and votes on
what the new fashion rules will be? So if that's the case
and the so-called fashion rule then why do they sell horizontal stripes in the fat people stores? I wouldn't wear
vertical stripes either—personally I think all stripes should
be banned. There, I just made a fashion rule; can I be on the
committee?

LAST FAT PERSON ON EARTH

Everywhere you turn there's talk about diets, losing weight, weight loss surgery. There are success stories about people who have lost one hundred-plus pounds. Every year *People* magazine highlights some of those success stories. You have friends that lose weight and while you are happy for them and wish that their weight loss would inspire you, somehow it makes you eat more.

Once you have friends that lose weight you feel a little sad or betrayed because now you don't have an eating buddy. Try going out to eat with your friend who has just lost weight. They will order a salad and water while you order something much too fattening. Sort of makes you feel like a failure, so you eat more. This is the way the game goes: the worse you feel, the more you eat.

It just goes to prove that you cannot lose weight until you're ready to make the change. It doesn't matter that your friends and family that surround you are doing it. It doesn't matter that you know you should do it for your own health. You have to do it for you.

You also have to be responsible for yourself and not anyone else. A snide comment was made to me that I didn't invite someone to be part of my weight loss club. It was said by someone who may have been feeling left out as I was making all these changes for and by myself. Reality check: there is no weight loss club. I'm on a journey to lose weight by myself and for myself. I have to be responsible for myself and watch what I eat. I cannot be taking care of someone else's dietary habit. I cannot tell you what you should eat; I have a hard enough time telling myself what I should be eating!

This is another reason why I've gained weight through the years; because I spend all my time taking care of everybody else, I forget about myself. So now it's time for me. If you want to lose weight, you need to find it in yourself to do it and be responsible for yourself and accountable to yourself. I will cheer you on, I will listen to you, but I can't do the work for you, I have to focus on me, and my own weight loss journey.

The desire to lose weight and better yourself has to come from within and what works for me may not work for you. My cousin is on her own journey, but she is doing what works for her. Her lifestyle is different than mine, she eats and exercises differently, but what she is doing for herself is working. No two people are the same, so no two diets are the same either.

I'm very happy for all of my friends and family who have been successful, but watching their success sometimes makes me feel like the last fat person on earth.

DINING OUT

Going out to eat is one of my favorite things to do. I love to experience new restaurants, I love being served and not having to clean up. But it can quickly turn into an uncomfortable experience. How many times do I have to stuff myself into a tiny booth? Who makes these restaurant booths anyway? It's only recently that I have learned to ask for a table instead of a booth. I don't know why it took me so long, maybe I was just too embarrassed to speak up and ask for a table. So by not asking for a table I would sit very uncomfortably in a booth. Recently I went to a Chinese restaurant and did my usual scan. I got nervous because I didn't see any tables. I asked the hostess, "Do you have a table instead of a booth?" she said, "The table area is crowded. Try this booth it is very spacious." She was correct, it was a spacious booth and I was thankful.

I walked into a restaurant with a party of six. They wanted to sit us in a large booth so I blurted out, "Can we have a table, it's just easier when someone needs to go to the restroom." That certainly is a valid reason. Why, with such a large group, should we have to inconvenience others to leave the table? The truth of the matter is I wanted a table so I didn't have to be squished into such a tight space, is that too much to ask?

If I were a host/hostess at a restaurant and saw a larger person walk in the door, I would offer them a choice. Would you like a booth or a table? Make them feel important and considered by offering them the choice. Seriously, you have to squeeze into these restaurant booths like a sausage. Now I have also recently learned an insider's secret from a very good friend who works in the restaurant business. If you are a large person and you cop an attitude with the person who seats you, they are going to sit you at a booth. To tell you the truth, I find that a bit funny and I hate to say it, but I think I would do it too, just to adjust their attitude. Maybe not all hosts/hostesses will, but those who want to prove a point to you will. It works both ways; when you are pleasant to the hostess when entering a restaurant, they will be more than happy to accommodate.

Now let's talk about those stupid tables at fast food restaurants like McDonalds where the chairs are attached to the table and you can't pull them out to sit. You have to stuff yourself into a tiny place that you clearly can't fit and don't belong. There are the few fast food restaurants that have those tables with the attached chairs and a (yes, "a" as in one) table with regular chairs. Chances are you'll go to get that table and it will be taken, by skinny people. Kudos to Wendy's restaurants because they have real tables and chairs. Don't laugh, these things are important to fat people. We want to be comfortable when we are dining out.

So once you are stuffed into your seat (and there is no getting up to go to the bathroom, you're in there for the long haul), the server comes to take your order, do you ever wonder what they think? Are they judging us about what we ordered? Do they walk away thinking, *They are going to eat all of that*? Or perhaps they are snickering because you just ordered a huge meal with a diet Coke. That even makes me snicker.

Even going out to eat makes us self-conscious about what people think about us. An evening out that should be fun and enjoyable becomes a stressful event, and we all know what being stressed out does to us... makes us eat more.

THERE'S ALWAYS SOMEONE FATTER

No matter how fat you think you are there is always someone fatter. That may sound terrible but it's true. And you are lying if you say it doesn't make you feel good to see them.

As I was stuffed into a booth at the Outback Restaurant wishing it hadn't been so busy so that I could have requested a table, my cousin poked me and said, "There's always someone fatter," and drew my attention to the next table. Yes a table, not a booth. They had my table, but it looked like they may have needed it more than I did. There was a couple that was twice my size (and I'm pretty big). It was like seeing old friends, I was so happy. Happy to know that I'm not the fattest person on earth, and not the last fat person on earth either.

What a vicious circle judgment is. We constantly walk around feeling judged by skinny people, yet we judge other fat people too. What is wrong with us? I suppose it is just human nature. I don't say any of this to be mean; I am one of the fat people. I've been judged, criticized, and made fun of, and it just makes me feel a little more normal to see other people in the same boat as me.

BEHIND THE SCENES (THINGS YOU MISS OUT ON)

Have you ever taken a good look at your family photo album? Where are you? Are you in the pictures or are you the one taking the pictures? I love taking pictures—of other people, that is. I want as few pictures as possible around of me looking like this. When I do have to be in photos, I grab a kid and position them in front of me to hide as much fat as I can. If there is no kid, I try to hide behind anyone and anything that is available to cover as much as I possibly can. This makes me sad because my children are growing up and there are very few pictures of us together. I should be accepting of myself and say, this is who I am. This is who my kids know and love. I know they love me for who I am, for the person that is on the inside. I know I'm a good person. But I hate the way I look, and I don't want photographic evidence. Once my weight loss journey is complete, it's going to take everything in me not to destroy the fat photos that do exist. As much as I will want to destroy them, I know that I will have to keep them around for posterity. I don't have many pictures of me with my friends, because I do not want to be in someone's photo album looking the way I look. But again, I'm missing out on having pictures of the good times we have. I have to rely on the memories in my mind.

I know this is all coming from me; it's my own mind, it's my own feelings. I know that my true friends look at me and see the person I am and not the outer layer. I know that in my heart. Still, I absolutely hate the way I look. Why do I want photos taken of me looking so ugly and fat? I don't. I want as few reminders as possible.

Have you ever stopped and thought about how many strangers' photos that you could be in? Out in public, on a vacation, there are families snapping pictures everywhere you turn. I have strangers in my pictures. Can you imagine them examining the photo saying, "Hey who's this fat girl?" And then you get cropped.

I was looking at some photos recently and noticed something that I hadn't noticed before. It was a photo of me watching my daughter play in a splash pad area. Sounds like a normal activity, right? Well, what caught my eye this time around was the stranger in my photo. There was a man standing nearby looking at me and the expression on his face was, "Holy crap look how huge this person is." Ok, so maybe you think that could be my imagination, but I saw it with my own eyes and I hated the way that made me feel. If I can see this in a photo, how many more expressions am I missing? I'd rather not know.

There's more to being behind the scenes than not wanting to be in pictures. There's so much you miss out on in life. I also won't go skiing, sledding, ice skating, or roller skating. I won't do anything that requires people to look at me, or any activity where I could fall. Something that I would absolutely love to do would be a "Trainer for a Day" at a place like Sea World but guess what... you are required to wear a wetsuit. I really doubt that they make a wetsuit that fits me, and on the off chance that they do, I think I may get mistaken for Shamu.

I avoid certain events, especially events that require you to dress up. I miss dressing up. I loved wearing dresses and skirts. I'm a girlie girl—I love fashion, skinny girl fashion of course, and I hope to be able to dress up again someday the way I used to. I avoid events like weddings and showers and my high school reunions. I have this great excuse for not going to any of my reunions. I say that the friends I had in high school are the friends I still have today, so why do I need to attend my reunion to see them? Truth is, I don't want to see anybody because I don't like the way I look. Another truth: the friends that I do have from high school I haven't seen in years because I'm hiding from them because I'm fat!

There are so many activities I want to try but being overweight prevents me from even dreaming about it. Things like ziplining, parasailing, and snorkeling sound like so much fun, but I just can't imagine myself doing them. Let's get over the fact that I'm a natural born klutz and have been known to trip over my own two feet (something I learned to laugh about a long time ago) but the fact that I am so overweight does not help at all. These things to me are for the thin and beautiful people, well mostly the thin and in shape. I've also never seen a large person parasail, is that even possible? Well, to answer that particular question, I did a little research on the internet. There was a travel blog and someone asked if there was a weight limit for parasailing. Of course there was a reply that said, "If you had to ask then it's probably not a good idea," but the real answer to this question is there is a weight limit. I did some research by calling around to a few of the parasailing companies and was told that the weight limit is generally 475 pounds. Good to know that even at my heaviest I could have gone parasailing. That doesn't mean that I would have. Our minds sometimes deter us more than our bodies do.

I know that I am fat and there are certain things I can't do, but my mindset has kept me from at least exploring options. I had never thought about calling a company to ask the question about maximum weight capacity to see if I was capable of doing something like parasailing. I just automatically crossed it off the list because in my mind I didn't have the type of body that I associated with the activity.

It's time to get out from behind the scenes.

FOR YOUR AMUSEMENT

Going to an amusement park should be something to look forward to, a day of fun with friends and family. However, even going to an amusement park presents issues for the larger person. The biggest issue for me is wondering, "Will I fit on the rides?" When I was thin, this was never a problem. I'd get in line, get on the ride, have a good time, never think twice about fitting on the ride and never give larger riders a second thought. It's only in recent years that I've developed this paranoia about not fitting on rides. It began in Williamsburg, Virginia at Busch Gardens. The quest was to go on every rollercoaster. My cousin and I were going to conquer every coaster in the park and at the end of the day get the T-shirt that proved it. As I was waiting in line to get onto Apollo's Chariot, I was watching as a larger lady had to get off the ride because the bar wouldn't go down due to her large stomach. I immediately started panicking, wondering if I would fit. It was too late now, I was next in line. I sat in the seat and to my relief the bar did come down and click into place. It was at this moment that I realized how uncomfortable I was on this ride and now began thinking, what if the bar comes undone and I fall out in the middle of the ride? What if I'm not secure in my seat because I'm oversized? I wanted to get off but it was too late. Thus began my panic mode every time I go to an amusement park.

One of the most embarrassing moments that ever happened to me was when my friend and I went to Six Flags in Massachusetts and we brought our daughters on the raft ride. We got on and went to buckle up. I had never had a problem on this type of ride, usually the seatbelts on the raft ride act in the same fashion as a seatbelt you would find in an automobile. To my dismay, the seatbelts on this particular ride hadn't been updated and wouldn't stretch far enough to click in. There was just not enough give. We were close to getting it to buckle but it didn't work. It was short just about an inch. We looked at each other in disbelief as the Six Flags staff member watched. We had no choice but to get off—our girls were little, and they didn't want to ride alone. I was mortified. The only thing that made me feel any better was that it wasn't just me. My friend was in the same boat (no pun intended). One would think that this would have made me want to lose weight, and it did for a short time, but I was back to my old habits before I knew it.

There is a lot of pressure to buckle up on an amusement ride. You have very little time. That certainly adds to the stress. There is not enough time to suck it in and figure it out; you are either in or not. Not being able to fit on a ride when your child is with you is mortifying. Your children love you so much and now they end up disappointed if they can't ride without you. That leaves you worrying how being overweight is going to affect their attitude. It makes you wonder if you've embarrassed them.

There was an almost incident at Hershey Park, Pennsylvania. We got a ride which had a type of T-bar. It was a tight fit, but I did fit. When the staff member made his rounds checking to make sure the bar was in place, he kept asking me if I was comfortable. This was his way of saying, "Lady I think you're too fat for this ride." I insisted that I was fine. There was no way in hell I was getting off that ride. I was in, the bar clicked, comfortable or not I was riding. I was still embarrassed at the same time because I knew what he was thinking.

I also had to be squeezed into a raft ride at Storyland in New Hampshire. The ride attendant had to come over and push the seatbelt down with all his might. To his credit he did it, but I was yet again reminded about my large size, which only made me want to eat more. Oh yeah, there were onlookers at this ride. All the people in line saw the whole thing, talk about wanting to die right there.

Through the years I have seen changes in amusement parks and the rides. The biggest change I've see is the signage. I'll never forget the first time I stood in line and saw a sign warning you that this ride is not good for people who are pregnant, have heart conditions, back or neck problems and—here's where the shock came in—may not accommodate all body types. Yes, I was shocked the first time I read that final line. It threw me right into a panic mode. That is the polite way of telling you if you are fat don't bother wasting your time in line. You won't fit and if you try to get on this ride and we have to ask you to get off, we've covered our ass.

I remember standing in line to get onto Mount Everest in Disney's Animal Kingdom theme park and reading one of these signs. I wanted to go on this ride so bad. I was praying that I'd fit. There was a sign around every corner warning me that I might not fit. I went into my amusement park panic mode. I started looking around in line to see if there were people fatter than me. There seemed to be a few, I figured if that person can fit, so can I. To my delight I did end up fitting. It was a tight squeeze and instead of enjoying the ride, I spent most of my time wondering if I was locked in securely enough. Because of these incidences, every time I get in line at an amusement park I look for people that are fatter than me and watch them get on the ride, so if I see they have no problem I can breathe a sigh of relief.

I will say that out of all the amusement parks that I've been to, the absolute best place for the larger guest is Disney World. The only ride other than Mount Everest that I have a problem with is Space Mountain. This is because the cars you get into are on the small side. I think this is because it's an older ride and when this ride was made there were no accommodations made for the larger guest. Other than those two rides, Disney World is a fat person's heaven; even the turnstiles accommodate the larger guest.

The other change that I've noticed take place over the years at amusement parks is that now many of them offer test seats right outside the attraction. Most of the seats are there unattended for you to try on your own. I have noticed that some of them have a staff member there to talk to you and assist you. I don't care for that method. If I'm going to try a test seat, I want to do it on my own; I don't want to have the embarrassment of not fitting in front of a staff member. I'm perfectly capable of knowing if I fit in a seat or not. I do like that they have the test seats; it prevents a lot of embarrassment.

I recently returned to Busch Gardens, Virginia. I was happy to see that they offered test seats at the entrance to every roller coaster. They were all unstaffed except for one. I wanted to try the test seat, but because it was being manned by two staff members I chickened out. I just wasn't at the point of handling the humiliation if I didn't fit. It takes a long time to get your confidence even as you are losing weight. I did try the seats that were unmanned. I was just much more comfortable, not to mention that I was with a friend of size and she was willing to try the seat first. The test seat had a red and green light. You pulled the bar down and if you got the green light you were good to go, if you got the red light forget about it. My friend got the green light and I was a little more willing to try it. I was nervous but I sat in the seat, pulled down the bar, and I got the green light too. So, after many years, I was elated that I could once again go on a roller coaster.

We did notice that the staff at Busch Gardens was very accommodating. There was a time when my cousin needed her bar checked and just needed a little extra push to get the safety to click and they were super sweet. They did not make her feel uncomfortable at all. I think they deserve an award for how accommodating and friendly and non-judgmental they were. As a larger person I sure do appreciate that.

SPEAKING OF TURNSTILES...

Turnstiles: another annoying inanimate object that can totally humiliate you. All the fun places have turnstiles that you have to go through before you can enter. Amusement parks and concert venues of course, those are two of the most frequented types of places during the summer months. Most of those turnstiles are a very tight squeeze. When I see them I go into a panic and say a quick prayer that I will not ever get stuck in one. One of the tiniest turnstiles I ever had to maneuver was at the Dunkin Donuts Center in Providence, Rhode Island—going to a concert, they will scan your ticket then you walk through the turnstile. It's a pretty tight squeeze and I don't understand why as they are not permanently placed. They can be moved to incorporate more space between them, so you would think they would space these out a little better.

There was one winter evening when I went to a show with my cousin. I had my coat in my hand as I approached the turnstile to have my ticket scanned. The lady working that particular turnstile who was to scan my ticket looked at me and asked if I'd like to go through the handicap entrance. I said hell yeah just so I didn't have to walk through the turnstile. She obviously could tell I would have a tight time with it. I had to wonder, did she offer me the easy way out because she knew I was fat, or did she think I was pregnant? It didn't really matter because I was just happy I didn't have to go through the itty bitty teeny tiny turnstile. It falls under the same theory of going to a restaurant and being seated by the host/hostess. If you see a person of size, offer them an option. So, I say thank you kind lady for giving me the option, it's a rare occurrence when someone offers me a more comfortable choice.

BOOB JOB

Looking back to when I was twenty-one, I had the perfect figure and some pretty good boobs (36 D's). I was well proportioned. As I slowly gained weight through the years, the boobs got bigger and bigger, (let's face it, there are only so many places your body will store the fat). By the time I had my second child the boobs were just gigantic, I couldn't even tell you what size they were. They were pretty darn big is all I can say. This certainly didn't help my self-esteem. I couldn't find bras that fit correct. I would have to order them by mail and they still weren't the right size. I'd be hanging out of them all over the place.

I know people talked about me behind my back, hell some people even talked about me in front of my back. I wanted in the worst way to get a breast reduction, but I was petrified. I was scared to death of surgery.

I'll never forget being at a birthday party for one of my best friend's daughters and overhearing her sister-in-law talking to her family about me. As I walked by I caught the end of the conversation as she was saying, "Well it can only be one of two things. It's either fat or plastic surgery." It was one of the most hurtful moments of my life. I had known this girl for years and I never liked her anyway—she was rude, classless, and not much to look at herself—but I would never (until now) say that in public. What I had just overheard had verified what I already knew about her. To know that there was a whole table of people sitting there discussing my boobs was beyond humiliating.

Again, I thought about surgery. But being the big baby that I am I quickly dismissed it.

I remember being at an event in downtown Providence. It was a racing event where companies designed their own mini race cars. There was a race and vendors and an awards ceremony. It was a lot of fun. As I'm mingling with people, I met a gentleman (I use that term loosely) who ran a hotdog stand and he was chatting with me. Being of the naïve trusting nature that I am, I did not realize right away that he could not take his eyes off of my boobs. He was so in awe of them he insisted we take a photo together. It was then that I caught on and I tried to refuse a photo, but he insisted. I can just imagine him showing that picture to all of his friends and the talk that was to be. That picture is probably hanging in his hotdog stand to this day. Really guys, there is much more to a lady than the size of her boobs. But I get it, they were pretty big, and if that made your day then so be it.

When I was pregnant with my daughter, I had a few friends that were also pregnant and the subject of breast feeding was a hot topic. Everyone I knew was planning on breast feeding. I never considered the option; my boobs were too big, too heavy, and I was too uncomfortable. I chose to bottle feed. My daughter turned out just fine for what it's worth. Not breast feeding was not the end of the world, but because I was so uncomfortable with my body, I felt it wasn't a choice for me.

A few years later while I was pregnant with my son, I was at the mall with my daughter. She needed to use the restroom, so I took her by the hand and walked through the food court. It seemed like the longest walk of my life. It wasn't busy that day and as I walked past the Subway sandwich chain, I saw the workers staring and then poking the other workers, telling them to look. Yes, that's right, look at the lady with the biggest boobs in the world walk by. Had I thought about it sooner, I could have joined the circus or a band of gypsies and made some money as a sideshow freak. It was the "Subway Moment" that finally made me decide that I was going to have the breast reduction. Walking by that food court sandwich shop was a life changing moment.

I was about five months pregnant with my son and I made an appointment for a consultation with a plastic surgeon. There it was, another humiliating experience... I had to stand there while the doctor took pictures. He needed to take them for insurance purposes, I understood this, but it didn't make it any less embarrassing. We scheduled the surgery for May; my son was due in February, so that gave me enough time to recover from my C-section. If I could have two C-sections I could have a breast reduction.

The timing was perfect because I was working a third shift job and worked by myself. Except for my coworker that I relieved when I arrived at night, there would be nobody there to even know I had the reduction, which had been a big concern of mine when I first seriously considered it five years earlier. I had thought of having it done after my daughter was born but didn't want to explain to all my coworkers. After all, it's not something I could have hidden; it's a very noticeable part of your body to have altered.

The night before the surgery I had a dream that I woke up from my surgery to find that the girls were still huge, and I was terribly disappointed.

The day of surgery arrived. I went into the hospital early in the morning. Here comes the Doc with a marker to make a "map" of where to cut right on my boobs. I could not wait for this whole ordeal to be over. I elected to have this done but there was tremendous embarrassment every step of the way.

They wheeled me into the operating room and when I woke up in the recovery room, I pulled forward my hospital gown and peaked down and said, "I have Barbie boobies." I was so excited. They ended up taking six pounds from each boob. I couldn't wait to go bra shopping. There were only a few people who knew I was going to do this. My husband, my sister-in-law, and one friend. All three of them took time out of work to help me as I had a brand new baby at home and I was not able to lift anything for a couple weeks. I was so grateful for their help. I was still on maternity leave, so I didn't have to take time out of work. The timing worked out perfectly.

My debut with the new girls was on my son's christening day. My mom who lived in Florida flew in for the christening and I had to tell her so she wouldn't be shocked; of course she was happy for me. The morning of the christening my brother and his family arrived at my house and my sister-in-law looked at my mother and asked her if I had it done. Everyone was surprised. I remember my aunt asking me why I didn't tell her I was going to do it, as she had one done many years earlier. It was just something so personal I had to just do it and not talk about it.

I've heard people who have had breast reductions say it was the best thing they ever did, and they wished they hadn't waited so long to do it. I can attest to that. It was worth it. I shouldn't have waited. I could have avoided a lot of humiliation.

However, that being said, people are just rude. It shouldn't matter what you look like or how big your boobs are, that should not give them the right to make you feel uncomfortable.

If you are reading this and have ever contemplated having a breast reduction, I am going to tell you it is totally worth it. Put your brave pants on and go talk to the plastic surgeon, you will not regret it. You too will wish that you had not waited so long.

ACCEPTANCE

There comes a time in your life that you finally have to accept yourself for who you are. Even before you start a diet or change your lifestyle you need to come to terms with who you are inside and out, good or bad. I never wanted to accept myself being overweight, I just couldn't do it. It was always, "Someday I'll do it, someday I'll lose weight," someday, someday, someday. I couldn't stand promising myself someday, I had to come to terms with who I was at that moment. So, who was I? Well, on the inside I was a good person: kind, thoughtful, generous, a heart of gold, I would do anything for anyone, a good friend, loyal and true. On the outside there's a different story. On the outside I was fat and unattractive; there is no other way to put it, that's what it was. I had to rely on what was on the inside to shine through. I came to accept this. I told myself if I never find it in me to lose a single pound, this is who I am; I have to deal with it. I know in my heart who I am, there's a good person in there. I will just have to deal with how people view me.

I was ready for it to end there. I was ready and willing to accept the fat me and move on and live my life. I was ready to quit trying to diet. I should have known better because

I don't give up. I have never given up on anything in my life and I fight for what I want. Once I accepted who I was at that moment in time, I became inspired to change my life forever. Sounds strange right? Accept yourself for who you are but turn around and change? I can't explain it. I gave myself permission to be fat for the rest of my life, but I didn't want that after all. It's almost like when a parent tells a child they can't have something and they want it even more, but once you let that child have it, they don't want it anymore. So, I told myself, go ahead, be fat, and my inner self said no, that's ok, I don't want to be fat anymore. That's why I think once you accept yourself for who you are, any positive changes you end up making will just be the icing on the cake. It just takes the pressure off.

If you want to go on the journey and lose the weight, that's great. Just as long as you are doing it for yourself. People can be cruel. You will walk down the street and people will snicker and make rude comments, children will point and laugh, but if you can accept yourself for who you are and learn to love yourself others will too. I've spent a lot of time worrying about what people think when they look at me and it's only recently that I've come to realize that people are not as shallow as we think. That realization came after my acceptance of myself.

While certain things about being overweight have caused many hurtful moments and some embarrassing situations, I always found ways to deal with it. It's one thing having to deal with it yourself, but when you have children that brings up other issues.

Before my acceptance of myself I always wondered, would my children be embarrassed that their mom is fat? I love my children so much and would never, ever want to cause them embarrassment, especially with something I have complete control over. I was always worried about what my children's friends would think.

What I have found is that my children surround themselves with wonderful loving friends. I will go into my son's classroom to visit and one of his friends will always come up to me and hug me. When my daughter has her friends over, I will come home from work and they all run up to me and give a hug and say, "Hi Mama Lisa." They don't care if I'm fat or not and that just melts my heart and makes me proud that my children have chosen such warm and loving people to spend their time with.

I have my own friends who I realize that when they look at me, they are seeing what's in my heart and in my soul. They are supportive and loving and I wish I could put into words how much it means to me that they see beyond the physical and see the person inside.

Once I finally accepted who I am and what I look like I became ready to make the changes necessary to better myself and go forward. Ask yourself this: if you never lose a pound can you learn to like yourself? It's a tough question; it will make you think about who you are and where you want to go. So, go ahead ask yourself that question and think very carefully about the answer, you may surprise yourself. Learn to love yourself for who you are right now, knowing that your inner self is much different than your outer self. Once you come to accept yourself, change will come to you much easier if you want it.

HIDING FROM FRIENDS

I have some friends that I haven't seen in a very long time, years actually. I started a second job and yes, the truth is working full time, working an additional job three nights a week plus weekends, and participating in the kids' school activities—dance, soccer, hockey, etc.,—leaves me little time for much else. The bigger truth is I've been hiding behind all of those activities. I look at this group of friends and I see beautiful, thin, happy, fun-loving girls. I feel inadequate. I feel like I don't belong in this group. I can't join in the conversations about fashion and exercise and things of that nature because they are thin, they work out, they go shopping and have a world of beautiful clothes available to them and I just can't relate or add anything worthwhile to the conversation. It's nothing that they ever did or said to me.

These are my friends. I know in my heart that they don't judge me, that they love me for who I am. But somehow, I've convinced myself that I am not worthy to be in their presence so I hide behind my work and I have let precious time slip away. I have let time go by that I could have spent with some very wonderful people and time that I will never be able to get back.

Yes, I'm busy. Yes, they are busy, but I sure find time to go to concerts with my cousin, and go to the movies with other friends, and once a month have a card night with another group of friends. The truth is the friends that I have surrounded myself with right now have only known me as being overweight. The friends that I am hiding from know me from when I looked my best. I never wanted them to see me at my worst. My current group of friends has become my cheerleaders; they know what I want to accomplish, and they are by my side. They look forward to me reaching my goal and give me daily support and encouragement and have been along for the ride from day one. I'm sure that my friends from my skinny days would be supportive as well, but why am I embarrassed to face them?

It's easy to create things in your mind and tell yourself that you're not good enough. I know this in my head, but it's so hard to believe in myself. I've spent so many years feeling bad about myself it's hard to move forward to a good place.

I refused to go to my high school reunion because I'm fat. When I looked at pictures that were posted on Facebook, I immediately regretted not going because I would not have been the only fat person there. Maybe I'll find the courage to go to the next one.

I wish that I didn't feel I had to hide from these people. Again, they never made me feel this way, I make myself feel unworthy. I know when they find out that I felt this way they may be hurt and may be upset with me and I know what they will tell me: they will tell me that I should have never felt this way and that they are my friends and would have been there for me. I will tell them that I know all of that, but I had to find my way back to who I used to be both mentally and physically.

The other day I received a message via Facebook from one of my best friends from high school. She wrote to let me know that she hadn't been on in a while and had just found my blog about my weight loss journey and said, "Maybe one of these days we can get together." I look forward to meeting up with her and picking up where we left off, but only when I'm at a comfortable weight. Again, what I feel comfortable. I'm still hiding, and I shouldn't be. Maybe when she reads this book she will understand.

CONGRATULATIONS! WHEN ARE YOU DUE?

We all carry our weight around differently. Me, I've got it all in my butt and my belly. Have you ever had someone walk up to you and ask you when you were due? I have and it's so embarrassing. This has happened to me countless times. When it first happened I wanted to die, and when my response to the person that asked was that I was not pregnant they were just as embarrassed as I was. I figured it served them right.

There was the time when I was looking at a house and the realtor looked at me and said, "Only downside to this house is that it only has three bedrooms," as she looked at my two kids and then at my stomach. My reply to her was three bedrooms were all we needed as we were done having kids. She didn't know what to say, served her right too.

One day I was standing in a restaurant waiting for my takeout order and the woman next to me asked me when I was due. On a whim I just decided to go with it. I replied, "In two months." I then got an earful about her pregnancy experience. It just seemed easier at that point to just play along. I was tired of telling people that I was not pregnant. It turned out to be a pretty comical moment. So that became my motto: just go with it.

There was another time when an elderly lady came into my office to pay a bill and asked me when I was due, so I just replied, "Soon." She came in every month for the next few months and asked me again. Finally after about six months she asked, "When is this baby coming?" and I said, "When it's ready." I thought she finally figured it out because she finally stopped asking. Not too long ago she came in again and asked me about being pregnant and I just couldn't take it any longer, I had to tell her I was not pregnant. That shut her right up, she had no words. Once I was able to quit the part time job I had to wonder if that little old lady would show up and ask whoever was there if I had left to have my baby. This woman obviously had no sense of time. I worked there for almost four years at that point so that was a pretty long pregnancy.

Another customer came in and asked when I was due. He was a jolly soul, pleasantly plump himself. I told him, "I'm not due, I just like to eat." Well, he had a good laugh and said, "Oh, you're just like me," as he pointed to his stomach.

The really embarrassing part of the customers commenting is that other people in the office clearly could hear this, though nobody ever said anything and I'm grateful for that. It sure does make me want to wear a button that says, "I'm not pregnant, I'm just fat!"

PLANES, TRAINS, AND AUTOMOBILES

et's talk about transportation. I've seen reality TV shows about people so large they have customize their cars so the seatbelts fit. I thank god that I have not had to go that far. That is for the extremely large person, I know. I have no problems in cars, well in the front seat of the car. I remember one time my sister-in-law picked me up and we had a full car, five of us. I got in to close the door and I had to make everyone in the backseat squish together so I could get the door closed. This was a small car, it was no Lincoln town car, but still, this is not normal. One should be able to get in the backseat of a car with two other people and be able to comfortably close the door, though in my defense the other two people were not of thin proportions either. Needless to say, we did not wear our seatbelts. We were packed in pretty good; if there was an accident, we definitely were not going anywhere.

I find trains to be a comfortable mode of transportation if we are talking Amtrak, but if we are talking trains as in subway types of trains or what people in the Boston area refer to as the "T," it is another story. The seats run a little small for the larger behind. During rush hour you are better off standing than trying to squish yourself between others.

The bus can present issues as well. If it's not crowded

and you can get a seat all to yourself, life is good. There were two women of the larger size who sat on a bus. One had a window seat, one had the aisle seat. It was during rush hour and there was an average size gentleman looking for a seat of his own. He came across the seats where the two women sat, leaving the middle seat empty. He took a look at them and announced, "I'm going for it," and dived right into that seat between the two women. Why is it that he had to announce he was going for it?

I'm sure by now the world is aware that airlines will charge a large customer for two tickets if they don't fit into one seat. I fly often and as time went by, the more weight I gained, the more trouble I had getting the seatbelt to fit. A few years ago, I sat down on my seat and went to buckle and went into my famous panic mode because I couldn't get the seatbelt to reach the buckle. I had it stretched to the limit. My daughter had to buckle it for me. I probably could have buckled myself if I didn't panic. After that incident I just couldn't take the stress of worrying if I would be able to buckle up on an airplane and I couldn't avoid flying altogether, so I did some research and I learned about the seatbelt extension.

The seatbelt extension is just that, it just gives you some extra room, it buckles into the existing seatbelt and you can ask your flight attendant for this. The next time I had to fly I knew that I could ask the flight attendant for one, but this was much too embarrassing for me. I didn't want to ask and have someone overhear me, nor did I want to be put in a position of asking for one and it turned out they didn't have any. So, I looked it up on eBay. I bought myself a seatbelt extender. There are several places you can buy seatbelt extenders online. There are four types of seatbelt extenders available: Models A, B, C, and D. I usually fly Southwest, so I purchased the type that they use.

Of course, now I gave myself another problem–I only fly

Southwest because I don't want to have to buy all four seat-belt extenders. I've limited myself to this one airline. But I tell myself it's only temporary because once I lose weight, I will never have to deal with this issue again.

So now when I fly, I go as far back on the plane as possible; most people want seats up front so this gives me a few minutes in a seat all by myself. I hook up my seatbelt extender before anyone can see. I sit back and am grateful that an embarrassing situation has been avoided.

I did some research on different airline policies. I went to their websites and found the rules regarding this subject listed under "customer of size." I had never heard that expression before. Because everyone carries their weight differently you have to research the airline's rules before you purchase your ticket. According to most guidelines you must be able to fit in the seat with the armrest down. If you can't you must buy an extra ticket. Southwest seems to be the only airline I've found that will refund you that extra ticket if the flight is not full. Some airlines like Delta do not require you to purchase an additional seat in advance, but will ask you to move if you infringe on another customer's space. They do kindly suggest you purchase two tickets to avoid this. I can't even imagine being asked to get off the plane to go purchase another ticket. I think I would die on the spot from humiliation. During my research I found that this policy had started when a passenger of normal proportions complained about a "customer of size" sitting next to her, stating that their "extra fluff" was infringing on her space. Extra fluff, yet another expression that I've never heard of before.

I am lucky enough to not have had this issue, but I'd just as soon lose this weight so that I don't have to worry about these things anymore. It's much too stressful for me.

I became so stressed out about flying and not having

the seatbelt fit that I thought about sending other people to pick up my daughter to bring her home from her summer visits to Florida. Even owning my own seatbelt extender, the mere thought of having to be buckled into any type of seat sends me straight into a panic mode. It has become a self-induced anxiety.

MIRROR, MIRROR ON THE WALL

The mirror is the most truthful friend you have. If you ask your friend, "Do these pants make me look fat?" chances are your friend is going to tell you no. Even true friends try to be kind; they don't want to hurt your feelings. Friends are under the impression that if they don't hurt your feelings, they are being a true friend. There are nice ways to tell someone that something doesn't look flattering on them, but not everyone has mastered that skill.

If you "ask" a mirror if something looks good on you, you can bet your fat ass that the mirror is going to tell you the truth. Have you ever asked a friend a question and they told you the truth instead of what you want to hear? I bet you got angry, didn't you? Or at the very least, a little bit offended and possibly stood there in disbelief thinking, *she really said that*? Well, I'm angry with mirrors. I hate their truthfulness, they make me feel terrible. Their honesty kind of sucks. Whose fault is it really, though? It's my own. I'm the only person who is in control of what I eat and what I do to my body.

I remember when I was thin I would spend hours in front of the mirror getting ready for dates. Going clothes shopping and enjoying trying on the clothes in front of the big mirrors in the dressing room. The three-way mirrors were especially fun. I also remember losing twenty pounds (back when I only had twenty pounds to lose) and trying something on for the first time and enjoying what I saw in the mirror. I liked mirrors back then.

Now, I avoid mirrors at all costs. I'm on mirror alert any time I'm in a store. As soon as I see one, I look away from it and hurry past. They say the eyes are the window to your soul, but mirrors are the window to the truth and I already know the truth. I don't need a mirror to show me how much weight I need to lose. I see it, I feel it, I don't need to stand there in front of a large three-way mirror that gives me a view that I find to be hideous. If I can't stand looking into a mirror and seeing myself, how can anyone else stand to look at me?

Sometimes I will catch a glimpse of myself in a department store mirror and say, who is that person? What I see in the mirror is not what I see in my head. In my head I try to convince myself that I am beautiful, and though I know I'm overweight I try to convince myself that it's not that bad. Then I see a mirror and the mirror tells me the truth. Yes, it's true, the truth hurts.

Mirrors just remind me of the way I used to look. How could I have let myself get to this point? Mirrors depress me, showing me every single flaw.

What if we lived in a world without mirrors, what would we look like? Would we care? It's hard living in a world where people are so caught up in beauty and vanity. The world doesn't care about the goodness in your heart unless you have a beautiful body that accompanies it. The first thing people notice about you is the way you look. It makes me sad to think about the young people out there that are overweight and how their peers judge them and make fun of them, and do not ever take time to get to know them.

HEALTH VS. BEAUTY

We all know that being overweight can lead to serious health issues, diabetes and heart disease among them. In fact, heart disease is surprisingly the number one cause of death among women. I wonder when people start diets what percentage of us want to diet because of health reasons or because of beauty and vanity. When I started writing this book, I vowed to be completely open and honest. If I'm being honest, I must tell you that I want to lose weight because of beauty and vanity. My quest to be thin has absolutely nothing to do with being healthy. Of course, I do want to be healthy, that goes without saying, but I am motivated by vanity. I know that by losing weight the health benefits will follow. I'm lucky that I am healthy. Other than being overweight I have no health issues. I also know that if I don't lose this weight now, I could very well end up with health issues. But, more than anything, I want to be beautiful. I want to look good. Remember Billy Crystal's character on *Saturday Night Live* saying, "It's better to look good than to feel good, darling."

Feeling good is great, I love to feel good, but more than anything I want to look good. I want to buy beautiful clothes, I want to walk into a room and have people say wow, she's pretty. I want people to come up to me and tell me how nice I look. We all want that. Everyone loves to get a compliment. This world is so focused on celebrity and which celebrity has gained too much weight and which one is too thin, who is the most beautiful person of the year. I feel hypocritical because I'm trying to raise my children to respect people for who they are and it's not all about looks, but how can I teach them that when I myself want to be celebrity beautiful?

What I wouldn't give to be as thin as Jennifer Aniston or look like Priyanka Chopra or Gal Gadot. I don't ever hear anyone say that they want to look like Rosie O'Donnell. Rosie has had weight issues to deal with like the rest of us. Maybe that's one of the reasons I respect her, she has followed her dream no matter what she has to deal with. Some of us use our weight as an excuse to not follow their dream and that includes me. Growing up I wanted to be an actress. My family thought it was a passing phase. I have never forgiven myself for not following that dream. It didn't matter if I failed or succeeded, I wanted the opportunity. My priorities changed and I didn't go after that dream, but years later I thought that maybe I could do local theatre and I did not do that either because I used my being fat as an excuse. In my mind, to even try getting into local theatre I need to be thin and pretty. I tell myself that perhaps when I lose weight, I will do it. There are many talented people that are overweight, but I have chosen to let my weight issues deter me.

Yes, I should be telling myself to lose weight for all the health benefits it would bring to me but I'm not. I'm much more interested in looking good in a tiny dress or a pair of tight jeans. Hey, at least I'm being honest.

FAT PEOPLE ARE FUNNY.

Have you ever met a fat person that wasn't funny? Or at the very least jolly?

Look at comedians, a good percentage of them are fat. I'm often told how funny I am. Yes, there are plenty of funny skinny people out there, but it seems that fat people have just a little extra something in the funny department. Is it because we have to find a way to be liked and we do that through comic relief?

Do we think people won't like us for who we are so we have to make ourselves funny? Is it easier to laugh at a fat person's jokes because they are funny to look at? Truth is many people will not have the pleasure of knowing who we are because they will take one look at us and move on, not wanting to get to know us.

Look at the kids at school. Standing in line waiting to be picked for the soccer game, the fat kid always gets picked last. That is unless they are the class clown and have won you over with the fact that they are funny.

How about a parent talking about their two children, one child being thin and the other being fat? The parent will say this about the thin child, "He is my smart one," and you know what's coming next about the fat kid, "He is my funny one." Now not every parent will do that, but I have witnessed it many times.

I have no facts or scientific proof on how and why fat people are funny, but they are. They just have a gift to make people laugh. I truly believe it's because we have to find a way to get people to see past the fat and get them to like us. How can you not like someone who makes you laugh?

SOME PEOPLE ARE NOT AS SHALLOW AS WE THINK

While I've talked about the people who won't give fatties the time of day and people who will judge you and make fun of you, there are good people out there who look beyond our physical appearance. I have always been so hard on myself that I didn't give most people a chance to show me that they are not as shallow as I thought.

I am very lucky to have found such a group of people that I can call my friends. These people have never once judged me. They have done nothing but support me and encourage me. They make me feel comfortable to be around them. I know when they look at me they see everything about me that makes me a good person. Everything on the inside, everything in my heart and my soul, they do not give the exterior a second thought. I don't think I have the words to tell you all how happy this makes me. I do try to find the words to tell them all how much I love and appreciate them for this.

My wish for everyone is that they can have a group of friends like I have found. These are both men and women and they have become some of my dearest friends. They have never asked me to change, they have accepted me for who I am. Though, because they know how important it is to me to change and to lose weight, they've joined my adventure and are along for the ride to keep me company.

All the times I worried about what my children's friends would think were wasted because they invite their friends to my home, and I have formed some close bonds with them. I know they just look at me as Lauren and Matthew's mom and nothing else.

Once in a while I will open up about my feelings on how I look to some of my friends and I've been told to never get down about myself. That is easier said than done, but I sure do appreciate that support. It's so good to know that for all the times that I have felt judged about my looks, I have these wonderful people in my life who don't care what I look like; they just care about me. They know who they are and if I haven't said it in a while I want to say it here in print where you will always be able to find it. Thank you, your friendship means everything and is helping to guide me down this road I'm traveling. I love you all.

Growing up in an abusive environment and feeling so unloved and unwanted makes these relationships so amazing and special to me. I'm forever grateful when someone looks at me and sees me for who I am inside.

So, I have learned that not everyone is shallow.

LET ME COUNT THE WAYS

There are countless ways to lose weight. Every year, January 1 rolls around and millions of people make their annual resolution to lose weight. I stopped this resolution years ago. It never worked, which is one of the reasons that I began a weight loss journey on December 17, because I did not want this to become a temporary resolution but a way of life.

Every year people sell their souls to Weight Watchers, Nutri-system, and Jenny Craig, among others. We hear ads on TV and the radio for new miracle pills. One pill a day and you don't have to change what you eat, guaranteed to block the fat. Then there are the weight loss surgeries. Now I have tried several diets and programs, including Weight Watchers, and out of all the plans out there I'm a believer in Weight Watchers. You eat real food and learn portion control. That's real life! It works but you have to make it work, you have to be motivated.

I have also tried Nutri-system and I'm not a fan of prepared foods, so that wasn't a good fit for me. It could be a good fit for some if you need everything done for you without thinking. From what I know about Jenny Craig, it's the same type of thing as Nutri-system, pre-packaged food.

Yes, I have entertained trying some of these programs but I chose not to, mainly because I didn't want to dish out the cash. Secondly, I am determined to lose weight on my own, my own time, in my own way. I must teach myself how to do this.

I have contemplated weight loss surgery, but I'm determined I can do this on my own. Surgery scares me. Not to mention I'm such a picky eater that I don't think I can follow the liquid diet you need to have in the beginning. I have friends that have lost weight through surgeries and I think some of them have lost too much weight. How you lose weight is a personal choice, but I believe the slow and steady route, teaching yourself how to eat, is the best plan to keeping it off.

I won't lie, the surgery option surely sounds enticing. I would do a little daydreaming about having it done and how quickly the weight would come off, but I just couldn't bring myself to do that. I did, however, tell myself that if I could not lose weight on my own that surgery may be my only option. It was just another little motivator to get my butt in gear and do this.

THE PICKY FAT GIRL

Fat people are some of the pickiest eaters I know. It's amazing we are fat because we seem to be so particular and peculiar with our eating. I know for myself my biggest downfall is sweets and desserts because I certainly don't tend to overeat on normal food. Well, ok, maybe every once in a while I'll have an extra plate of pasta, but normally I'm over-indulging in the desserts.

I have a friend who eats no sweets or dessert but will eat a whole roast or corned beef in one sitting. Just the meat, no side dish.

I used to work with a guy who only ate four items, one of them being pizza and it had to be from a certain place. I'm pretty sure that when his large pizza was delivered for lunch, he ate the whole thing by himself. That's a lot of pizza for one person.

I know for myself, there are just so many things that I won't eat. I know after people offer me things to eat and I say I don't eat this, or I don't eat that, they must say to themselves, "She's pretty picky for a fat girl."

The list of things I won't eat is long. I'm not a big meat person. I like a good steak out at a restaurant or if I make one at home, but it has to be a rib-eye and the way I spice it up. Anyone else tries to make a steak without my spices, I don't want it. Chicken must be boneless and you can keep the legs and thighs, I can take or leave a pork chop, ribs need to be boneless and with BBQ sauce. Hamburger, well, again, I'll only eat them at certain restaurants. I'll eat them at home but not usually enjoy them.

I'm not an adventurous diner. I won't eat ostrich, bison, venison, frog's legs, or anything else of that nature. I won't drink milk or eat eggs. In fact, if I go out for breakfast I limit myself to French toast, waffles, or pancakes. On a rare occasion I will order a breakfast special because I will feel like having toast, home fries, and bacon, but I will ask them to keep the eggs that come with the meal unless someone else at the table wants them. At that point I will ask for those eggs to be put on a separate plate because I don't want them touching my other food.

I don't like my food mixed, such as shepherd's pie, which if you've never had it is a one dish meal made with hamburger, corn and/or peas, and mashed potato. It's layered. I don't usually eat it, though a good friend of mine made it and hers was very good, but I will not ever go anywhere and ask for this dish. Needless to say, I don't care for many soups because again, I don't like my food to be mixed. Perhaps that's why I'm not a huge fan of pizza. I'll eat pizza but it's never my first choice.

The extent of my seafood menu is lobster, crab, shrimp, scallops, and on a rare occasion when I'm really in the mood, scrod. I will not eat tuna, swordfish, bass, trout, sushi, or anything else that has gills.

And dare I talk about vegetables, how about corn, squash, spinach, cucumbers, carrots, lettuce, and peppers (oh and mushrooms). Those are what I like. I know it's terrible and I really should eat more veggies. I learned something recently about myself on that point. I've tried so many times to eat salad and I don't enjoy it. It occurred to me one day that it's the lettuce. I started making my salad with everything you would put in it minus the lettuce and I didn't mind it, it took almost thirty years for me to realize I don't like the lettuce.

I'm just as bad when it comes to fruit—a very limited list, which does not include honeydew melon, cantaloupe, kiwi, etc. Give me a pineapple, a grapefruit, cherries, and an occasional banana and I'll be happy. I'd love to order a fruit salad when I go out, but they load those up with honeydew and cantaloupe and I just don't like it.

So, by now you're asking, what does she eat? And if she barely eats why does she have weight issues? Well, aside from what's listed above, I'll eat bread, pasta, sandwiches, and I've never met a dessert that I didn't like.

So, let's see, I think I've diagnosed my problem. It's not a mystery it's... CARBS. Yes, too many carbs, not enough fruits and veggies, not enough protein. Way too much of the bad stuff. Now that the nutritional part of the equation has been solved, I can work on that.

I'm not going to wake up in the morning and suddenly love fish and cauliflower, but I can be more aware of taking the things I do like and eating more of that and cutting back on the carbs.

I'd like to tell you that I'm going to try new foods, but I can't. I'd be lying if I sat here and said that. I know me and I know that I'm stuck in my ways. There are things I'm willing to change and things I'm not. Things I'm willing to give up getting to my goal and things that I refuse to do.

Let's face it, I'm a stubborn Italian and I'm a female so there's no changing the fact that I'm picky. I will always be picky. I just need to learn how to make picky work for me. Perhaps I am missing out on trying new foods, perhaps someday I will open my mind and take an adventure outside of my comfort zone, but for now I will make my picky eating habits work.

LYING ABOUT YOUR WEIGHT

I recently went to renew my driver's license and it hit me: for more years than I can remember I have lied about my weight. I'm one of the most honest people you will ever meet. You always know where I stand, but when it comes to my weight, I can't even stand to hear it said out loud. For many years my license has stated that I weigh 175. When I went to renew it this year, I had to fill out a new form and I chose to put my goal weight on that form instead of the weight I am now. I can't explain why I did this. When you present your license to someone, do they really look at the weight? And how would they know if that was your real weight or not? And why would they even care?

There have been times in the past when I started a diet and lost interest but didn't want people to know. So, when they would ask how I was doing... I lied. I would say I lost a pound here, a half a pound there. Not only was I lying to my friends, but I was lying to myself.

There was the time when I was working for a radio station and we had gotten an advertising buy from a product called Metabolife. It was a weight loss pill. I happily volunteered to try it out. I was excited... a miracle pill to help me at last and I didn't have to pay for it, all I had to do was go on the air and promote it and tell everyone how I was doing. At first it was great and I did lose a little bit of weight. Like all my previous attempts I got bored and didn't follow through. I was still bound to this contract, so I had to go on the air and lie. I made it up as I went along; I'd tell the listening audience how great this product was, and I would add a pound or so to my weight loss every week or two. Of course, the people that saw me every day couldn't even tell I was losing weight. I lost weight alright, in my mind. I eventually had to drop out of the program because it clearly wasn't working. I wonder how many bottles of pills were actually sold.

GOING BACK IN TIME

I've always said that to understand any adult you need to go back and examine their childhood. Many weight issues stem from those days of youth that should have been easy and carefree. We can only hope that all children grow up in a loving, supportive environment. That is not always the case. It wasn't the case for me.

Recently I took a drive past some of the places I lived as a child. Many memories came flooding back. Things that I had blocked out for so long were right there like it was yesterday and I'm sure there are so many memories that are still repressed.

I remember having to get up and get ready for school on my own, having to walk to school and because there was never anything for me to eat for breakfast, I used to take a little detour into a convenience store and steal my breakfast. Of all the things available to steal I chose cottage cheese. I would sneak it into my bag and when I got to the playground at school I would go off to a corner and eat it. From my recollections I enjoyed having this for breakfast, but as an adult I won't touch the stuff. Gee, I wonder why? I often wonder if I really got away with shoplifting or if the people who worked at the store knew and just felt bad and let me do it. Really, who steals cottage cheese? I think if I worked at a store and saw a kid steal cottage cheese, I'd let them get away with it too. I would think you have to be desperately hungry to steal cottage cheese.

The stealing of cottage cheese led to a further life of crime. I remember walking home from school and stopping at a different convenience store. It was very crowded, packed with schoolmates, and I grabbed a handful of candy bars, stuffed them in my pockets, and left. The cashier gave me a look so I'm pretty sure she knew. I never went back to that store, I was too afraid to get caught.

Then there was the time that I was playing on the side of my neighbor's house. Their window was left open and I peeked inside. There were shelves full of baking items and the item that caught my eye was a bag of chocolate chips. I wanted them so bad. Knowing there was nobody home, I opened the screen and climbed into their home and ate a few handfuls of chocolate chips. I was very careful to put the bag back exactly as I found it, or so I thought. Somehow, they found out about my little excursion into their home. I was in big trouble. I did have guilt about it for a long time because they were nice people, they were always very kind to me. I soon realized I was not cut out for a life of crime.

When I think about the few times I ventured to open the refrigerator door in my own home without permission when nobody was around, the only item I ever remember being in there was a package of bologna. That is another item I will never eat again. I'm sure there must have been other food, but I just can't ever remember seeing the refrigerator full. All I remember is that package of bologna staring me in the face and how disappointed I felt that there was nothing else.

There is a list of things I'll never touch, and perhaps this is where my pickiness came from. I was served stewed tomatoes on Sunday morning and if I was lucky, I would get a Pillsbury biscuit with it. That Pillsbury biscuit almost made the stewed tomatoes worth eating. What the heck are stewed tomatoes anyway? Open the can and put it in a bowl... I don't think that was what they were intended for. Dinners consisted of Spam (fried spam—I don't think you can get grosser than that), fried hamburger with onion, and on a good night would be pancakes and bacon. Vegetable of choice was always lima beans. Gross!

We moved to Florida for a brief time and had a grapefruit tree as well as a kumquat tree in our yard. These were good days as I could just go and pick the fruit off the tree whenever I wanted. When I had to walk to the store for my birthmother I had to walk right past an orange grove, and even though I knew I wasn't really supposed to pick the oranges off the trees I did anyway. It was a lot better than stealing cottage cheese and there didn't seem to be anybody lurking around watching either. This was also around the same time when I came home from school and was told that we were having steak for dinner and it turned out to be liver. Again, what more can I say than GROSS! Add all of this to the list of things I will never eat again as long as I live, and the good news is nobody can make me.

I remember spending weekends with my grandmother. That was a treat! When I was at Gramma's house, I could eat whatever I wanted, whenever I wanted, no questions asked. I remember sometimes I would eat a whole Sara Lee cheesecake over the course of the weekend. It was the total opposite of my day to day life. And Gramma made the best homemade macaroni and cheese. I could open the refrigerator and help myself any time I wanted and I could ask for anything. I wonder how much she knew about what went on at the other house. It must have been hard for her to sit back and watch and wonder. It was a drastic difference going from a home where I ate what I was served and was afraid to ask for food to being able to have whatever I wanted. This was likely to be the beginning of my eating problems as there was no continuity.

Summertime was the best with Gram when she would rent a house on the lake the first two weeks of July. She'd bring me with her and it was amazing, swimming and day trips and playing games of solitaire. Sitting on the front porch watching fireflies and eating bowls of cherries. The vacation quickly ended, and it was time to return home. I would get so sick to my stomach on the way home just thinking about having to return to my everyday routine, living with a mother and a stepfather who had no idea how to love a child and who had no idea how they were shaping this child's future. I'm thankful that I had those days with Gram; she gets a lot of the credit for how I turned out in this life as she had such an influence on me. I wish I had told her that before she passed away.

Eventually I moved in with my dad when I was a teen. This took some adjusting in many areas, including the food area. I came to live with Dad and found that I also had two younger brothers. One of whom had his own weight issues. Coming from a place where I had issues with food, I had to figure out how this all worked in a new home. Here the refrigerator was always full; there was no shortage of food. There were always leftovers from dinner. These leftovers sometimes became problematic. Sound strange? Well, let me tell you there were many fights over who got the leftovers.

I was the first one of the three of us kids to get home. I came home one day looking for a snack, I knew we had some leftover stuffing (one of my favorites) so I heated it up and enjoyed. About an hour later, my little brother comes home and goes to get a snack... and he starts looking for the stuffing. When I said that I ate it he got very upset and didn't talk to me for a few days because I ate *his* stuffing.

We can laugh about it now but back then, this was some serious stuff.

There was also a time when one brother didn't speak to the other because he had eaten the leftover soup. An interesting side note to this story is that just recently I was hanging out at a friend's house when I got a text notification on my phone. When I went to see who it was, I saw that it was a message from my brother saying, "I finally forgive you for eating my soup." I replied that it wasn't me who ate the soup, I ate the stuffing. He responded, "I forgive both of you." This has been something we've joked about for many years. I asked him why he was finally forgiving us. He responded, "I've grown up and I wanted to make you laugh," and he did indeed make me laugh.

We were always battling over food. Dad would bring home a package of cupcakes. There were twelve in a pack; this meant we all got four. I would take my four and hide them in my bedroom. If I ate them all and my brothers had some left, I'd eat theirs too! (My life of crime continued I guess) Of course, this led to the famous, "Who ate my cupcakes?" fight. I would never tell that it was me. Why I did this I just can't explain, but it was the beginning of no self-control.

When I turned fourteen, Dad told me I was too old to go out for Halloween. I still had to take my brothers though. I was resentful of this; I had already lost out on so much of my childhood, I couldn't understand the "too old for trick or treating" rule. Lucky for me, I got home from school before they did and would raid their candy bags. Again, this would cause fights over who had been stealing their candy, and I couldn't possibly admit it was me (The life of crime continued).

Then there was the time that I made Dad mad because I counted the potatoes on everyone's plate and was upset that my brothers had more potatoes than me. I don't remember what happened in the end, but I know that Dad couldn't believe I sat there and counted all the potatoes.

So yes, there were several issues in my childhood that I can use as an excuse as to why I've gained weight over the years. However, you can only blame your childhood for so long.

As an adult only you are in control.

MY CHILDHOOD

I wasn't going to write about my childhood, but I realized that if I'm going to be honest, and if I'm going to fight the demons and win, that I do need to talk about it. It's part of who I am. It's what made me who I am today both good and bad. It's where my issues with food began. Putting it out there and facing it head on once and for all is where the issues with food will end.

I don't know all the facts, as we all know there are three sides to every story: his side, her side, and then the truth. I can only relay this as I know it. What I know is this.

I was two years old when my parents divorced. The reasons why they divorced are not relevant. This is what I know: I know that I was kept away from my father. I don't know how old I was when the last contact with my father was as a young child but I did not see him for many, many years, until I was about eleven. I have been told that my birthmother dropped me off one night at my grandmother's house. Gram was supposed to be babysitting for the evening; the story has been told to me that one night of babysitting turned into a year as my birthmother had taken off to Texas with her new boyfriend. I'm not sure how old I was, maybe four or five, but one of my earliest memories is being a flower girl in my birthmother's wedding to this new guy. I remember her wearing a red dress, which leads me to believe this wedding may have been near Christmas time. After that I remember being told that her new husband was going to adopt me.

Jumping ahead to the courthouse on the day of the adoption, I remember walking in and seeing my dad standing up against the wall. At the time I wasn't sure it was my dad as I had not seen him for a long time, but I remember looking at this man and intuitively knowing it was him. I remember the judge asking me if I wanted to be adopted and I remember wanting to say no but feeling like I had to say yes. I don't remember what my life was like prior to that adoption, but all the things I can remember happened once that piece of paper was signed. It almost makes me believe that I was okay before then and once my stepfather adopted me he felt he could do whatever he wanted to do.

There are so many blanks in my life from childhood. It makes me sad sometimes because I have no stories to tell my children. I have nobody to tell me stories of my childhood. The things that I can remember are not pleasant. Sometimes I wonder how I survived. Sometimes I have flashbacks and have to question myself if these things were really real, but then I look and see I have scars both physical and emotional that will be there forever.

My behavior didn't seem to matter; no matter how good I was, nothing I did was ever right. My stepfather was brutal and my birthmother was just as bad as she had her own hand in my abuse, both by physically contributing and by standing by and letting this guy torment her daughter. As a mother myself I can honestly say I would never let my children be treated the way I was. I often wondered why this person wanted to adopt me in the first place, was it a big act? Was it so that he could have control over me because a little piece of paper legally made me his daughter?

What can a young child do that is so bad that he/she has to be beaten with a belt, hit, punched, pinched, and more? One of the worst punishments I can remember was having to stand in the corner with my arms straight up in the air, and sometimes I would have to hold a Tonka Truck above my head. When it got too heavy and I wasn't holding it up straight, things were thrown at me: shoes, batteries, whatever was handy.

Of course, there was being hit with and without belts, there was being pushed and lifted up in the air by the shirt. One time my stepfather lifted me up in the air and dropped me on the cement floor of the basement. I remember waking up in my bed. I must have hit my head so hard on the floor I was knocked unconscious. There was no visit to the hospital to see if I was ok, and it was never spoken of again. I don't even know if my birthmother knew this happened. If she did know what the hell was wrong with her for letting this go on?

I remember being about six years old and my birthmother completely freaking out because she couldn't find her keys. Screaming at the top of her lungs she demanded me to help her find them. I remember her standing in the dining room with her hands on her hips and looking at the table and like children do, I mimicked her actions. I stood next to her with my hands on my hips looking just like she was doing. The next thing I knew she was screaming at me that the keys weren't going to find themselves and she hit me so hard across the face that I fell. Unfortunately for me, where I was standing when I was hit was the front of my bedroom, and when I fell I hit my head on the metal corner of the bed. I ended up with a cut across my left eye. It must have been pretty bad because I never saw my birthmother show any emotion when I was hurt in the past and this time she was a little unnerved. She brought me to the hospital where I had to get stitches. I also remember thinking at that time that she must love me after all because she was upset and brought me to the hospital. I think about that now and that is pretty messed up. Looking back, I wonder if she was upset because she thought she'd be reported.

Now this delightful couple had a child together, and while I was the evil stepdaughter, this baby grew up to be the prince and could do no wrong. Even he was allowed to hit me all the time. I could never really blame him as he was just a little boy learning what his parents taught him. There was a time where it was my job to keep him entertained. We were outside playing and he had a rocking horse that was on springs that would bounce up and down. I was too big to go on it and was told to never do so. It so happens that my little brother demanded that I get on that stupid horse. I told him that I was not supposed to go on it. He said if I didn't go on it he would tell. Well I knew what would happen to me if he told them that I wasn't keeping him entertained, so I got on that horse. As soon as I did he ran into the house and told my stepfather that I was on it. So damned if I do, and damned if I don't. What happened next was pure torture. My stepfather asked me if I was on the horse. I tried to explain but he didn't want to hear it, so he punched me in the stomach and said "Go to your room." I tried to go to my room and he punched me again, and said, "I told you to go to your room." This happened over and over for several minutes. What a very sick person, telling a child to go to their room while purposefully not letting that child get up off the ground to actually get to the room. I finally was able to escape to the solace of my bedroom where I cried myself to sleep after wishing I was dead.

It was more than the physical abuse. There was never any love shown, never any hugs or kisses or kind words. I craved these things more than anything. I just wanted to feel loved. Later in life I found comfort in food, but as a child searching for this emotional fulfillment, I had to find other ways to get me through my days. I spent hours on end in my room living in a fantasy world that I created. I was probably about ten years old when I created my own escape world. I gave myself a father (who was remarkably similar to actor Sylvester Stallone) and two brothers (who resembled young actors at the time, Emilio Estevez and Charlie Sheen).

If you read that last sentence carefully you will notice that I did not give myself a mother in this fantasy world. I never did. It was only recently when thinking about this that I made that connection. I felt so betrayed by my birth-mother that even in my fantasy world no mother existed. Sometimes the story would be that the mother died, or the mother left, but the mother never had a face or a name. In this fantasy world that I created I was loved and adored and protected, I was treated like a princess. I spent hours on end creating warm and cozy family scenes in my head. I created scenarios where I was picked on by people (which was not far from the truth) and my brothers would come to my rescue. I felt safe in this make believe world and every night when I would go to bed I would create new stories in my head, always with these three actors, and that is how I would get to sleep. I can't tell you why Sylvester Stallone, Emilio Estevez, and Charlie Sheen were my safety net, but they were the chosen ones and they helped me survive.

When I wasn't busy in my make believe world I spent my time listening to music and reading books. Anything that would take me to faraway places, away from my harsh reality.

I dreamed of running away to become an actress who was famous and loved by all. I'd perform for myself in front of the mirror. Like Cher, I'd be so famous that I would not need a last name. I'd only be known as Lisa. Probably because I didn't want to have the last name of my stepfather, and because he adopted me, my last name given to me at birth was nonexistent for me.

I never had any friends until I moved in with my dad and went to junior high. It was a combination of moving around so much (I went to six different schools in one year) and not having time to make friends, and other kids knowing I was different and probably just not liking me, as well as not being allowed to have friends. I don't know why we moved so much, comments were made that perhaps my stepfather was in some sort of legal trouble but I really don't know. I know that we moved all around the state of Rhode Island and to Florida and to Texas. I remember one time being out in the yard and a little girl came over to see me and my birthmother called me into the house. She only let me back outside when the little girl left.

I remember one time living in a two family house and there were some college kids who rented the top floor. They took a liking to me. They were very kind. On my birthday that year they came down and knocked on the door wanting to see me to give me a gift. I remember hearing my birthmother tell them I wasn't feeling well; that was a lie because I was in my room playing by myself. They handed her the gift and much to my surprise she gave it to me. I opened it and still remember to this day it was a gift set of Love's Baby Soft body spray. That gift meant more to me than anyone will ever know, other than my grandmother. I can't remember getting gifts, well, not gifts that I got to keep.

I cannot remember my birthday being celebrated at all. I cannot remember one single party. I do remember that I was supposed to have a party when I was turning six, just a small party, grandparents and aunts, no big fuss, no school friends; after all, I didn't have any. The party was cancelled because I had the measles. I cried so much my stepfather's sister, who was always very kind to me, asked me why I was crying and I just said I didn't know. The real reason was I was so excited that I was having a party and I knew it would never be rescheduled. I was promised that we would reschedule it, but that never happened, just as I had already predicted. As I remember this event, I'm wondering whose idea it was to have this party after all. I'm thinking it was probably my Nana (Nana was my stepfather's mom) as it was to happen at her house.

I think my birthmother and stepfather kept me away from as many people as they could so nobody would find out what really went on in our household.

Even the best times of the year were ruined. Christmas morning I would wake up to presents under the tree. I would open them, we would go to my Nana's house, Nana would ask me what I got for Christmas, and it was one of the few times I would speak. For a brief moment I would be a normal child as I ran through the list of what Santa brought. The next morning we would be returning some of the items that I received. I never understood this until I was much older. I remember waiting in very long lines and not really know why we were there. I think my birthmother would return the gifts and keep the cash. I remember one year getting a small typewriter and I loved it. We brought it back to the toy store the very next day. When the clerk asked the reason for returning it, she said it didn't work. Most parents would be exchanging the broken item for a new one if that was the case. Mine just kept the money. I never got a replacement.

Then there was the time when I got a toy that could make creepy crawly bugs. It sat on the top shelf in my closet for a very long time, because I was afraid to ask to play with it. I would have had to ask someone to get it for me from the top shelf that I couldn't reach. I went to my cousin's birthday party and he opened the gift from us and it was the same toy I had in my closet. I told him, "I have that too," and then something clicked. I went home, I looked in my closet, and my toy was gone. I put two and two together. My birthmother had taken my toy from the closet and wrapped it up for my cousin. Now, she could easily argue the fact that it sat on the shelf in my closet for months and that would be true, but I was afraid to ask someone to take it down to play with. And the fact that it was mine, a gift to me, well, I just couldn't believe that a parent would do that to a child.

It all started to make sense. Just like the time there were kids outside my house roller skating and I remembered I had skates in my closet. I was so excited I was going to get to do something the other kids were doing. I ran into the house, went into the closet to get the skates, and they were gone. Yep, another one bites the dust. I just stood in front of that closest feeling so deflated.

When I turned eleven I was brought to a lawyer's office where I saw my father and his wife for the first time since I was very young. Arrangements were being made for me to go live with my father. I was ecstatic on the inside though I could not show it. I moved in with my dad and found that I had two younger brothers. I was very excited for a fresh start in life. They had made a nice bedroom for me, my own TV and stereo, they took me to buy new clothes. I felt safe and secure for the first time ever.

Unfortunately, my dealings with my stepfather and birthmother were far from over. There was some legal issue between my stepfather and an employee of his that he had fired and I had to go to court, at eleven years old, and testify. I can't recall all of the details as to why I was involved, but my dad was going to bring me to court, the arrangements were already made.

The evening before the court appearance, I was in the shower. I was happy, singing along to Billy Joel songs, and I heard the doorbell ring. It had to be about seven or eight in the evening, I thought how odd for someone to be coming to the house that late. Even at eleven years old, I was intuitive. I had a bad feeling about how the rest of the night was going to turn out. My dad's wife knocked on the bathroom door and told me that the police were there to take me back to my birthmother. Saying I was upset was an understatement. Up until that moment I didn't want to talk about what when on in that household, and I begged them not to take me. I remember saying, "Show them the scars on my back." There was nothing anyone could do. I was brought to the police station where I waited for my birthmother to pick me up.

In the car on the way home, she promised after court I could go back to live with my dad. I believed her. The next day after my court appearance she badgered me all day long, asking me why I liked living with my dad and why don't I want to stay with her. I kept insisting I wanted to go back to my dad's until I just couldn't take the badgering anymore. She wore me down and I said, "Fine I'll stay with you." At that point she promised things would be different. Would you be surprised if I told you they weren't?

When I turned thirteen things got drastically worse for me. What I'm about to tell you is something that I've only told to two or three people in my lifetime. It's one of the most painful things that's ever happened in my life and I will not go into all the details; it's where I have to draw the line with my transparency. I've dealt with it. I only bring it up because it's part of my story. Just thinking about this event still upsets me.

My stepfather brought me upstairs to an empty room; my little brother followed us up there. My stepfather sent him away. At first I thought I was going to get a beating—for what I don't know, I hadn't done anything, but then again, I never did have to do anything to deserve it. Once he sent my brother away, my gut told me I was in for something else. I could take you to the house, to the room, and to the very spot that I was standing in because it is etched in my mind forever. I had never been so scared in my life and at that point I was almost wishing he'd hit me because that was something I was familiar with.

He must have been reading my mind because he told me not to worry, he wasn't going to hit me but what he wanted to do was explain to me that I was getting older and he wanted to explain sex to me. I wanted to die. I was young and naïve and had no idea what that meant. He explained it alright, and that's where I just can't tell you anymore. I just can't go back there. All I can say is that it's not exactly what you think, but it was bad enough and it was embarrassing enough. I remember him telling me that he was going to take me to the doctor's and get me birth control. I knew I was in big trouble and I knew I had to get out of that house.

I had not seen my dad since the night that the police took me away, but I found his phone number in the white pages and I skipped class to call him. I don't know how it happened, but the next thing I know is I was being told that I was going to live with my dad for good. My little brother was sitting on my stepfather's lap and he looked so sad knowing I was leaving, I will never forget that face. My stepfather looked at me and said, "Are you happy now, you're leaving your brother." My heart broke for him but I knew I had to go. I had to get out of there once and for all. I had to protect myself and it was all instinctual. Shortly after that my stepfather and birthmother were dropping me off at a lawyer's office with five paper bags full of clothes and walked out the door without saying goodbye. I didn't even get to take my books or music or the few toys that I had. I sat there and waited for my dad to come and get me. After that I spent so many years worrying about my brother and wondered how he turned out.

My dad had to adopt me—how messed up is that?—I was adopted my stepfather and now my birthfather had to adopt me back. His wife adopted me as well. So, a little known fact is that I've actually been adopted three times. My life was so much better. It was not without adjustments of course.

I went from a house where I had to hide and stay out of sight, where I did not speak unless spoken to and where I ate only what was given to me, to the total opposite. There was a family who did things together, there were hugs and kisses and I love you's. I was invited to participate in conversations and I could eat whatever I wanted when I wanted. All I had to do was open the refrigerator door.

These issues are just the tip of the iceberg. As I said, there are so many things that I've blocked out and really don't want to remember, and it's okay. I know people reading this must be wondering if I've seen a therapist; yes, a few times in my life I have. Did it do me any good, no. I do not wish to sit there and talk about these things with a random stranger. I do believe therapy can help people, I'm not against it, but my therapy is talking with my friends and writing this book. The memories of my childhood are painful and the hidden memories can stay hidden as far as I'm concerned because there is no reason to bring them up. Like I've said, I've only brought them up now because it's relevant to why I've gained weight over the years. I know that all of these things contributed to my state of mind and helped make food the only thing that I could count on and the only thing that made me feel better for many, many years.

The irony of saying that the food made me feel better is that overeating actually made me feel worse about myself in the end. Yes, while I was eating all that comfort food and eating away the pain I was also gaining weight at an alarming pace, and in turn I created so many other issues that I am dealing with now.

It was bad enough that I had self-esteem issues from everything I dealt with as a child, but by packing on the pounds I created deeper ones. It took me a very long time to stop feeling sorry for myself and, as strange as this may sound, embrace what I had been through. By embracing it and coming to terms with it by telling myself, this happened, you turned out ok, you were lucky enough to have enough good people enter your life that were positive forces and good influences. The old saying is true, what doesn't kill you makes you stronger. If I can say so myself, I am one of the strongest people I know. That is why I know I will not fail during this weight loss journey. I am lucky enough to have people believe in me and I never had that before.

Getting in touch with my dad when I did was my survival instinct. I knew I had no other choice. Lucky for me I listened to my gut. Moving in with my new family normalized my life. Even though I finally had stability, I still had to sort out my feelings about the past. I blamed my birthmother for so much. I felt that she chose a man over her child. I hoped and prayed that if she ever found the courage to leave him she would contact me. I learned years later that they did indeed divorce. I would be lying if I said I wasn't hurt. At the very least an apology would be nice, but even with that... it can't take away the things that were done.

I had some contact through the years with my grandmother (my birthmother's mother) up until she passed away. I went to the wake to pay my respects as she was a huge influence in my life. I was contacted by my aunt (my birthmother's sister) who was always one of my favorite people. She told me that the family wanted me to come and that my birthmother would be there of course, but she would stay right by my side. I was very nervous; it had been over thirty years since I'd seen her, the woman who gave birth to me, but I had to go for my grandmother, and for my aunt. I arrived at the funeral home and as promised my aunt was right by my side. I went through the receiving line and was happy to see my uncles, who I hadn't seen since I was a child. I came face to face with my birthmother and it was like looking at a stranger. I politely shook her hand, offered my condolences, and moved on. Once I finished walking through, I was surrounded by my cousins and I was so grateful. My stay there was brief and I left. A small part of me had wished that my birthmother would say something to me, but I knew it wasn't the time or the place.

I have to admit that I felt awful about myself. I hated the way I looked. How I wished I could have walked in and come face to face with her as a thin and pretty person. All the things that she had done to me and the things that she had watched me go through, and all I could think about was how fat I was and what she must think. That has to tell you how much self-confidence I had: absolutely none. I drove home thankful that it was over and I haven't seen her since.

More recently I found my little brother through Facebook. He seemed happy to hear from me. I told him that I had never stopped thinking about him and that I had hoped he would have contacted me years ago. He thought that I wouldn't have wanted him to. We exchanged a few messages and I haven't heard from him since.

I've moved on from those memories that haunted me in the past. I'm on my way to conquering this battle with my weight once and for all. I finally believe that I deserve to be treated with respect. I finally respect myself and with every pound that melts away I become more and more self-confident. Though I would never ever want to relive my past, nor do I wish it on anyone else, I accept it for what it was and understand why I am the person that I am today.

CHANGING LANES

Life in the fat lane... I've talked about the reasons of how I ended up in the fat lane, I've talked about things that happen while you're coasting along in the fat lane. Now it's time to talk about getting out of the fat lane.

As I've said before, for so many years I put the happiness of others before myself. Always doing the right thing, always doing what was expected of me, always trying to please everyone around me. I was always trying to be the perfect Daughter, the perfect Wife, the perfect Mother, the perfect Sister, the perfect Friend. It's a lot of pressure to try to be so perfect in everyone's eyes. I spent so much time trying to do what everyone wanted me to do and not doing what I wanted, not doing or saying things that made me happy. I would bend over backwards to make others happy and make them feel important and I never got that back in return. Little by little I was losing who I was inside and out. Eventually I felt like my happiness didn't matter.

Now we can sit here and debate about who put that pressure on me to be so perfect. Was it everyone around me or was it myself? It's like the fine line between love and hate... it's really hard to tell sometimes. I suppose that I have to take a big part of that responsibility. Nobody told me to try to be perfect, I had an image in my head of what perfection was and I wanted to make that reality. I like to refer to it as Norman Rockwell Syndrome. I had been through so much crap in my life I just wanted everything to be picture perfect. By trying to create the perfect world it was my own self that set the bar so high.

Something I don't know how to do very well is say no. If someone in my inner circle needed something, they knew they could call me. I'm the person in everyone's life that can be completely counted on and trusted. Do I like to be this person, absolutely! But being this person that was there for everybody all the time came at a cost. The cost was not paying attention to myself.

For years I've wanted to lose weight but why couldn't I? I would join Weight Watchers and quit, join again the following year and quit; this was a cycle I could not break. Every time a friend would start a diet, I would join in too thinking that this was the magic I needed to finally do it. I would play Jedi mind tricks. If a friend of mine got pregnant, I would think great, for nine months she will be gaining weight and I'll take this time to lose all the weight I can. I still couldn't do it. I just couldn't stick with anything. Sure, everything I tried worked for a short time. I would lose interest, I would be bored, I would get busy, and yes, I would just stop caring.

Losing weight has always been in my reach so why haven't I been able to obtain the dream of being thin?

December was the month that I made my mind up for good. The idea of this book had been floating in my mind for a year. I was tired of being the idea girl. I would always come up with ideas and never follow through. It was time to take action. That morning I stepped on the scale and saw a number that I did not like. That was it, my mind was made up. I needed to get my act together once and for all. I needed to stop thinking, stop dreaming and do it. Call me crazy but who starts a diet right before Christmas? I do! I've always been a little crazy... there she was... the fun crazy girl I remembered. I knew if I used the "holidays were coming" excuse I would just be putting this whole process off and it would be months before I would think about it again. No time like the present. I decided that this was it, the moment of truth. I would lose this weight once and for all and never look back. I would start writing my book and I would also start a blog about my weight loss journey. That's a lot to tackle all at once (that's me though, all or nothing) but I was determined and there she was again, a little hard to recognize because I haven't seen her in so long but slowly she was revealing herself. The old me, the one who had big dreams and thought anything was possible.

I've been in the fat lane for so long and I refuse to stay there any longer. I'm changing lanes. I will not consider it a diet but rather a journey. We all know food is going to surround us forever so it's learning how to deal with it. It's learning how to enjoy it and when to indulge and when not to. It's learning how to find exercise that you like and doing it and then doing a little extra when you do overindulge. This is the hard part. This is what I have to do on my own. Nobody can help me with it. It's not going to be easy but I'm more determined than ever. I'm more motivated than I have been in a very long time.

As I sit here today writing this chapter (in the kitchen of all places) surrounded by the aroma of what I was raised to call gravy and most Americans will call spaghetti sauce, (homemade of course) I'm so close to my first goal. Since my life changing moment on the scale in December I've lost a total of twenty-four pounds. That elusive one pound is what I need to mark a major milestone.

I've made this journey public. I've started my blog; I share the blog on Facebook and I have my inner circle that knows what I'm doing. There is a reason for this. The more public I make this journey, the less room there is to fail.

Imagine going through all this trouble only to fall back into old habits and not completing the journey. Not only would I be disappointed in myself, but think of how disappointed Team Lisa would be. There is no room for failure.

GETTING RID OF
NEGATIVE WORDS

When the kids were little, I had a bad word list, words that I viewed as derogatory or negative. Words like hate, stupid, dumb, etc. The reason for this was to teach them how to be positive. It's time that I take my own advice. I've decided to use the same method for myself. Let's start by getting rid of the word CAN'T. Thinking and saying, "I can't do this is," not allowed. I CAN do this, I'll throw away the word can't, I'll throw away won't as in it won't work. There will be no more feeling sorry for myself—ok, so I gained weight, yes, a lot of weight but that's in the past. Focus on the future. Remember the goal. Will it be hard, yes, but the old saying no pain no gain will prove to be true.

A good friend once told me that you can accomplish anything; it's all in your mind. It's true, I am retraining my mind. I will no longer give the power to the negative words. Negativity spreads like a cancer, but I have also seen what the positive can do. Positivity can be just as powerful as the negative. It's easy to get caught up in the negative, it's much harder to stay positive. Once you embrace that positive power it really turns your life around and is just as contagious. Wouldn't you rather walk around upbeat and happy than miserable? Remember it's all in your mind.

HAPPINESS IS NOT FOUND ON THE BOTTOM OF THE PEANUT BUTTER JAR

Sometime ago I developed what I thought was a cure for any bad day. It was the Peanut Butter Cure. You take a jar of peanut butter, add a bag of chocolate chips, mix it together, and stand in the kitchen eating it right out of the jar until you feel better. The thing is that I got to the bottom of the jar before I felt better. When it was gone, I felt worse than when I started. Happiness eluded me yet again.

Let's talk about being happy, as so many people are overweight because they are not happy. I found that it's a vicious circle. You're not happy so you eat. You eat and you're still not happy. You gain weight and this causes you to be even more unhappy with yourself. What are you not happy about in your life? You need to find the root of the problem. Until you self-examine and find what is causing your unhappiness you can't move on.

We've all heard the saying that you need to love yourself before anyone else can love you. I believe this also applies to happiness and losing weight. You need to be happy with yourself. You need to find out exactly what you are unhappy about and change it. It's time to take charge and stop blaming others for making you unhappy. Sure, people are going to upset you. You'll have a bad day at work, your boss will piss you off, your other half will annoy you, you will have stress—it's not a perfect world. You need to learn how to turn all of this into a positive. Stop and think... will this thing that is upsetting me matter a week, a month, or a year from now? If the answer is no, then shake it off, better yet, go exercise it off. I have the best workouts when I'm upset.

The journey to a thinner you starts with a lot of soul searching. So many of us have tried "every" diet, been on again, off again the diet train for many, many years. Happiness has a lot to do with it. Put yourself first for a change. Make yourself happy.

Another saying that I've heard over and over again within the last few weeks from different sources is, "When the student is ready, the teacher will come." This saying is so true; when you are truly ready to make a change you will find the tools and support right there in front of you just waiting for you. I've asked myself about all the times I've tried to lose weight and just wasn't committed to it, why? Why wasn't I ready before? Why have I started this journey and been so committed to it, more so than I ever have been in my entire life?

We all know this would have been easier to do when I knew I was only ten, twenty, or thirty pounds overweight. I spent so much time being miserable about my weight. I became so unhappy with myself, and that spilled over into other aspects of my life. I think that before you can truly start a weight loss journey you have to come to accept your fat self. Accept yourself for who you are at this very moment. Imagine that at this moment, the way you look is how you are going to look forever. Decide to be happy with that. Now anything that you do from here is going to be a big accomplishment, you will be thrilled with every ounce that you lose. Before starting this new way of life, I accepted who I was. I was fat but I remembered who I used to be, no, not the thin version of myself, it went deeper. I remembered how much I used to laugh and love life, and adventure and fun and hanging out with family and friends.

It was the inner me that I had lost, and once I accepted that fact that the outer me was only a small part of who I was I felt okay. I realized I can change the outer me, but the person I had been hiding and wanted to be resurrected was the inner me. Once I accepted who I was, I was ready. Ready to make the improvements I needed to.

I have spent too much time worrying about making others happy instead of myself, thus making myself miserable. Going out of my way to always be there for others, always putting others' needs first before my own. I put too much pressure on myself to be perfect and act perfect. Now don't get me wrong, I love doing things for people. I have a big heart, I'm generous and thoughtful, I'm a natural born pleaser. I will bend over backwards to put a smile on someone's face; that will never change, it is who I am and it is what people love about me. But what does need to change is I need to make myself happy, I want to please myself. I am important, I matter, and I deserve to live life how I see fit. I'm finally starting to see myself as others see me and realizing what a good person I am.

I had gotten so wrapped up about how I looked and how people viewed me, especially people I didn't know. Who cares what strangers think? They don't know you. Why spend so much energy worrying about it? Why spend so much time even worrying about what the people who do know you think, if they are not accepting of you for who you are then they really are not your friends.

I remember when I first gained a lot of weight, I was chatting with a girlfriend and she made a comment to me that her husband said something about, "I've never seen her so fat before." As she started to say this she paused and seemed to have changed the way she said it, it was as if she was telling me that he said that about her. This bothered me for a long time. I was very positive that they had been talking about me. I wasted so much energy thinking about that one comment and it turns out that this person really wasn't my friend at all. When I went through a crisis in my life, she was nowhere to be found.

Negativity is contagious and for so long I was angry, depressed, and just basically unhappy because I wasn't happy with me. Now I have not turned into a Pollyanna; nobody can be happy every minute of every day, but what I'm saying is it's what you do with those emotions when you have a bad day.

In the past I would try eating those negative feelings away, never feeling any better when I was done. So no, happiness is not found in the bottom of the peanut butter jar, happiness is found within you. The hard part is dealing with people around you. People can be mean and thoughtless. Some have said some terrible things to me, things that I won't soon forget because they were so hurtful; words can make you feel invaluable and unimportant. Nobody knows you better than you know yourself. Only you know what you are willing to tolerate from people. You need to surround yourself with good people. I know it's hard, but cut loose the negative forces in your life.

It can be difficult to get rid of all negativity because maybe the people you work with can be negative or perhaps they are family members and you are just stuck with them. If that's the case, then you need to be the one to teach them how to treat you. People treat us the way we let them treat us. This is all easier said than done, I know.

We all need to be surrounded by people who will not judge us, who will support us and encourage us. Sometimes, I feel like I get more support from my bra than from certain people in my life. I've learned to keep these people at a distance and only deal with them when I'm in control. I'm learning to stick up for myself and teach people how to treat me. Just because I'm a good person doesn't mean that people can walk all over me and treat me badly. If I let them, then that is my fault.

When you are doing your soul searching and weeding out the negative forces think about this: Imagine you're holding a big sifter (kind of like one that you would use when panning for gold) then imagine you are throwing all your friends, family, and coworkers in there. Gently shake it back and forth so that the negative ones will sift through. Now, who is remaining? Who are the golden people in your life? These are the people you need as your support group.

The people who remain in the sifter should be the most positive people you know. Surrounding yourself with them will make a world of difference. They will be your encouragement, your cheerleaders, your true friends. When you have a bad day, they will not feed you negative advice but lift you up with positive reinforcement. We all deserve to have positive forces around us. It becomes our responsibility to make that happen.

For me it was easy to identify things that made me unhappy. I was unhappy because I let myself get out of control for so many years; I've been unhappy because I was fat. Prior to that there were things that made me unhappy, so I ate. Food was my friend. It was bad relationships, it was a bad childhood, it was not putting myself first and feeling unimportant. I've since identified these factors and started working on ways to make every aspect of my life better.

For some it's not so easy and the reasons lie deep, counseling may be the way to go. I tried counseling and it didn't work for me. I am not one to sit and tell my issues to a stranger. I'd rather sit and talk to my family and friends who know me. But be aware of who your friends really are; some friends will just agree with you and tell you what you want to hear, other friends will be brutally honest with you.

It's the brutally honest friends that you want to help you. It will be hard to take sometimes because after all we are only human, and we like when people agree with us and tell us we are right. We are not always right, and we need to hear it. Keep the people you trust close by. If you choose to talk to your friends and family rather than a counselor, be sure that you can trust them completely. Many times I would confide in a family member that I thought for sure I could trust, and they broke the trust by telling someone else. It will always get back to you. That's when you want to reach for the jar of peanut butter, and it will start all over again.

Oh, and please refrain from having an all-night talk session with the friend who will hand you the jar of peanut butter.

THREE MONTH CHECK IN

It's been three months since I started my journey on the road to thin. To this date I've lost thirty pounds and gained many new habits. I watch my portions, I don't snack during the day, I eat fruit, I only drink water, and the biggest new habit of all, I exercise. I exercise almost every night. I walk, and when I walk it's at least three miles. I work out with games on the Xbox, I use an elliptical machine. I've never been more committed, or more proud of what I've accomplished. Has it been easy? Well I'm happy to report so far, it has. I think because I was really ready this time and it wasn't forced, I just started doing it. Now I know the more I lose, the harder it will get, but so far, I've been having a lot of fun doing this. It doesn't mean that I don't have bad days and wouldn't love to go to the store to buy a few candy bars and eat them all at once. But more than ever, I'm ready for this mentally. I've learned how to talk myself down from situations where I want to binge. And I have people I can call to help me if I need it.

I am over a fourth of the way to my goal of one hundred pounds. I am down to a smaller size and my confidence is growing.

I've learned to set small goals and reward myself with things other than food. A movie night, a new outfit, etc. In fact, I bought an outfit in a smaller size and within a week the pants were loose. It's a good dilemma to have.

The scale is no longer viewed as the enemy, it's becoming a friend. A friend that I visit every morning. It's important to me to weigh myself every morning even though they say to only weigh in once a week. I feel more in control doing it every day.

I don't deprive myself. I eat what I want; I just control the portions. I have given up a few things, like when I go out for Chinese food I don't eat egg rolls anymore; I don't love them enough to want those calories. I've not had ice cream in the last three months. I don't feel ready to have it as it is a big weakness, though I have replaced it with pudding.

I'm treating every day as an adventure and making this journey a fun one.

The weight I've lost is a huge accomplishment that I'm so proud of, but there is something else that I'm even more proud of at this point. It appears that through my own journey, talking to other people and blogging, I've actually inspired others. So many people have come up to me and told me how what I've been doing has inspired them to lose weight, to exercise, and I've been asked to keep on blogging and talking about it. This journey has become more rewarding than I've ever expected.

WHO SAYS YOU CAN'T HAVE YOUR CAKE AND EAT IT TOO?

I've tried many different diets, many programs, and have even considered weight loss surgery. I have had friends that had the surgery. I have some that have done a gastric bypass and some that had the lap-band surgery. Seeing how quickly their weight fell off was very seductive. I did the research. I have decided against it. First of all, I'm a big baby. I hate needles, I hate hospitals, and I seriously lack the confidence that I could handle the surgery. From what I read you have to be on a liquid and soft diet for several weeks. Many people I talk to say they can eat whatever they want in the end, but it was a comment that a friend of mine made when I posted a picture of a birthday cake on Facebook that really got me thinking. She commented how beautiful the cake was and then said, "I miss cake."

When I saw that comment, I just couldn't imagine going to a birthday party and not having a piece of cake. I'm the kind of person who wants it all! Everything in my life has come to me the hard way and by hard work. When I'm committed and passionate about something it's all or nothing. I've made the commitment to change my lifestyle and lose weight, but I believe I can have my cake and eat it too; in fact, I have. There is no reason why you have to give things up forever unless you truly want to and won't be bothered by it. I love Chinese food and I have chosen not to have egg rolls anymore, but that doesn't mean that one day I won't want one. If I do, then I'll have half, but for now I'd rather eat my calories in other ways.

While on this weight loss journey, I have been to several birthday parties. Sometimes I'll refuse cake and sometimes I'll have a tiny piece. There are many factors to this decision. I think about how close I am to my next goal, I ask where the cake is from; if it's from my favorite bakery well yeah, I want a small piece but I make sure it's a small piece, not a giant piece like the old me would have. This is ok; this is eating and living normally. After I have that cake, I make sure I get my exercise in.

You do have to identify your problem foods. We all have them; for me it's ice cream. I have learned to deal with it because I'm not willing to never have it again. I'm also not willing to ever have a weight problem again. I must find the happy medium. The key is moderation, exercise, and a little planning. If I know I'm going somewhere, and I choose to give myself permission to have a treat of some kind, then I will plan accordingly and add some extra exercise into my routine.

If I'm going out to dinner that night, I'll eat a lighter breakfast and a lighter lunch knowing that I'm going to go to my favorite restaurant and enjoy something that may have a few extra calories.

Choices and accountability will allow you to succeed.

ICE CREAM IS MY KRYPTONITE

Everybody has their weakness—Superman had Kryptonite, I have Ice Cream, so I found it extremely funny that someone told me I was melting away like an ice cream cone, talk about ironic.

Ice cream is my most favorite treat in the whole entire world. I could eat it every day, morning, noon, and night. In fact, in the past, I have been known to have ice cream for breakfast. As a kid, every so often Dad would take us out to the movies and stop at an ice cream shop for dinner. Ice cream for dinner, every kid's dream. I've done this with my own children from time to time. You can have so much fun with ice cream; you can have a backwards dinner, which is ice cream first and dinner as dessert. When my kids have sleepovers, we will have a midnight ice cream buffet: three different kinds of ice cream to choose from, with many toppings and whipped cream.

Think back to when you were a child, I'm willing to bet that one of your fondest memories is playing in the street on a hot summer day and hearing the joyful noise of the ice cream man coming down the street. Still to this day, I love to watch the kids go running outside when he comes. It's a rite of passage.

There are so many varieties and brands, it's never ending. You can have it in a bowl, in a cone, or eat it out of the carton. I certainly can't be the only one that has ever taken the pint of ice cream and sat in front of the TV and said that I'll just have a little and bring it back up during the commercial. Problem was that the ice cream never made it back to the freezer.

You can get ice cream in a pint, a gallon, at the market, at a local ice cream shop, on a stick or as a sandwich, hard serve or soft serve. It's the most perfect dessert ever. You can eat it in or get it to go. It's portable, you can even eat it while you're driving.

This very well could have turned out to be the longest chapter in this book as I could sit here and write for hours about ice cream. I won't give it that much space as ice cream is one of the culprits for my weight gain. I will, however, find a way to live with it. As much as I love ice cream, I know I will love being thin even more. I am determined to find a way to coexist with ice cream peacefully.

ISN'T CHANGE WHAT
IT'S ALL ABOUT?

We all say that if we won the lottery, we wouldn't let it change us. Reality check—it would absolutely change you. Some for the good, there are people out there who would do wonderful things with that money, and some for the bad, those who become greedy, selfish and spoiled.

Same thing applies with weight loss. You start out thinking you are just going to lose weight, but you don't think about how the whole process will change you. After all, isn't this what it's all about... change? Changing your lifestyle, eating habits, and your appearance? You learn new things, including new habits, and as the pounds drop, a new you emerges and you become more confident. You feel better, happier, and in my opinion it's your true self that emerges. I say that your true self emerges because you can change habits, but people don't tend to change their core personalities. You are who you are.

Three months into this new life I was told by a few people that I was different, and they could see changes in me other than my weight loss. Most of them commented on how they were positive changes, that I had a more positive outlook, I was happier. But with each positive reaction, there is always a negative reaction. It was brought to my attention by someone that my attitude had changed and not for the better. The way it was said to me made me think that I appeared a bit selfish and self-centered. Very far from the person I really am and those who know me well know that's certainly not the case.

To this type of reaction, I simply say that the person that you see emerging is the person that has always been there. What you used to see is actually the person that was hiding behind the fat and the unhappiness. So, I guess to you I have changed.

Some will recognize that this is the old me. Those who didn't know the old me won't recognize me and will either love me or decide that maybe I wasn't the person that they thought I was and that will be their loss. Yes, I have changed—I have become happier, more confident, and my old fun personality is shining through. To me what is most important is that I like myself. If I met me at a party, would I want to become friends with that person? The answer is ABSOLUTELY!

SIX MONTH CHECK IN

It's been six months. I can hardly believe it. Total weight lost is forty-seven pounds. The first three months brought the fastest weight loss; it's slowed down a bit since, but I'd say an additional fourteen pounds is not too shabby. I have three more pounds to hit the halfway mark. This is very exciting. Though the weight loss has been slower these past few months I'm ok with it because I have never been on a diet this long. Then again, this isn't really a diet, it's a lifestyle adjustment.

I am still exercising regularly, still drinking my water, still concentrating on portion control. Summer is just about here; the weather hasn't been all that cooperative for my walks and I find that I really enjoy walking much more than being inside on the elliptical machine. I've increased my walking path. I haven't mapped out the miles yet, but I bet it's at least four miles now.

Staying focused has been easy, but what has not been easy is shopping. I can't wait for the day when that gets easier. I need new pants and shorts I just can't find anything that fits right. So, I've resigned myself to using everything from last year, and though most of the shorts and pants I have are a bit baggy, I'll just have to deal with it. Tops on the other hand are a different story. I actually went to Macy's "normal size" department and bought a shirt. That was exciting. I've been pulling tops out of my closet from last year that were too tight and have been able to wear them. In fact, someone asked me the other day, "How many tops do you have?" I replied, "More now since I can fit into my old ones."

I get up every morning and do my hair and makeup, something that I went a long time without doing just because I felt so lousy. I would brush my hair and put it in a ponytail and that's about all the prep work I was willing to do. Now I curl my hair every day, I put a full face of makeup on; I feel girly again. It's still hard to look at myself in the mirror. I suppose it will be for a while.

I have found that I can be in some pictures. Of course some photos are better than others and I'm still ultra-picky about what I let the public see, but I've actually been able to post a few on Facebook and feel good about it. My mom told me that it took my brother a few minutes to recognize me. That was a good feeling.

My bathing suit from last year fits better, it's a tad bit big in the boob area but what the heck. I don't really feel like spending money on a bathing suit I'll only get two months use out of. I have spent several weekends lying outside tanning, again something you wouldn't catch me doing for many years.

I feel good! I have so much positive energy and am really putting the time into my appearance. All of this seems to be really showing to the outside world because I've been told that since I've started this journey I've been glowing.

I made a personal goal that for every fifty pounds I lose I'm going to get a tattoo. I'm six pounds away from that first goal. I'm excited and nervous at the same time. But this is how I keep going, by setting small goals for myself.

I finally had ice cream for the first time, and though I did enjoy it I think I've finally come to terms with my weakness and don't feel the urge to splurge any longer.

So, I will continue on and look forward to reporting my progress in my nine month check in.

CHINESE BUFFET

The Chinese buffet, best bargain for your money. You get lots of choices; remember how much we love choices? You don't have to choose just one dish, you can have them all. Why don't we have Italian buffets? If there was an Italian buffet restaurant I would have loved that too, but we don't have any of those. Now that I think about it, in the area that I live there really are no other ethnic buffets, I wonder if they have them in other areas? What we do have here is an abundance of Chinese buffets.

I've made it clear that I love to eat, and I love to eat out. One of the places that I used to go to often was the Chinese buffet. Why not—it was fast, easy, cheap, something for everyone; you don't have to wait for your food, it's already prepared. It's a fat person's dream. Eat all you want. And that's what I did. When you go to the Chinese buffet you need to get your money's worth, so be sure to eat as much as you can. Yes, that was the mentality of the old me.

Once the weight loss journey started, any thoughts of going to an all-you-can-eat Chinese buffet were tossed out the window. Not the kind of place that anyone on a diet should be. I was successful in avoiding this scene for several months until the kids asked to go, and I would say no way,

I can't have that. They were understanding at first, but one night they just begged and begged to go. I decided I would attempt this; after all I'm the one on a diet, and why should they be deprived. I've been doing great and I need to learn how to handle all situations. So, we hopped in the car and headed off to the Chinese buffet.

It's funny how my attitude had changed and visiting this establishment was an eye-opening experience. I was very careful in my choices. Well, as careful as I could be, there are not many healthy choices available here. I certainly did not eat half has much as I used to. I was no longer worried about getting my money's worth. What really surprised me were the things I noticed as I was walking from the buffet back to the table.

I stated that the Chinese buffet was a fat person's dream, well, let's make that a fat person's paradise. It's the only place you can go and absolutely gorge yourself on as much food as you want. As I walked back to my seat, it was a surreal experience. I saw so many overweight people sitting at their tables (some were so overweight they didn't even fit on their chairs) their plates in front of them piled high with food, and we all know that they wouldn't be stopping at just one plate. This overloading your plate syndrome I just don't understand. You can get up as often as you like, so why pile the food on your plate in the shape of Mount Everest? Really... if you are eating at this particular establishment, you're certainly not embarrassed about how much you will be eating, so why not just make several trips. By the time you reach the food on the bottom won't it be cold?

I'm not judging, I'm just observing, I was there too. I just couldn't help but think that months ago when I was on the other end there must have been someone taking this very same walk looking at me and looking at my plate, thinking the same thing I was thinking.

I no longer enjoy going to the Chinese buffet. I will go on occasion because I'm invited to go with friends, or the kids want to go. I'll have a few of my favorite things, but I can't eat like I used to nor do I want to. I'd just prefer to go to a non-buffet establishment where the portions are controlled.

NEVER FORGET WHERE YOU CAME FROM.

It's advice that I tell my children all the time. No matter where life takes you, no matter how much money you make, no matter how successful you may become, never forget where you came from.

This is something I want to follow as well. I come from a small town in a small state. I spent the first thirteen years of my life in an abusive environment. I didn't grow up in a rich family. I've worked hard for everything that I've ever had from material things to relationships.

When I reach my goal of being thin, I will not forget where I came from. I will not forget that for many years I was a fat person too. I will never judge another human being for what they look like.

I can't deny though that when I do see someone who is overweight my heart breaks because I can only imagine what they have been through in their life. I know what I have been through and everyone's journey is different. I can't help but see those who are so large they need to use a scooter to get around because they can't bear their own weight, and I want to help them. I know all too well that you can get to a point in your life that you just give up and say I'm okay with being overweight and this is just the way it is.

I know that I was almost there. I know that I almost gave up. I know that I was actually considering the weight loss surgery and told myself that I had to try this on my own one last time. I did not want to have surgery and I gave myself the ultimatum–do it on your own, be successful this time, because if you don't you have two choices: live life large or go for the surgery. Those were not very good choices. Those options were not good enough for me.

I will not forget where I came from and if you read this book and see me on the street and you want to talk about it, I invite you to do so. Going through this journey makes me want to help others. I hope I get the chance to do so.

WHEN FOOD NO LONGER RULES

We all have a relationship with food. Like any relationship in life, some have a very healthy relationship, and some don't. Those who don't tend to have an abusive food relationship. Food is needed to live, but somehow we have turned it around so that we live for food. I'm not denying that sometimes it is just plain fun to eat, like hanging with a good friend. For a very long time food was my friend, it was the friend that I turned to when I wanted to celebrate or when I needed to drown my sorrows. Food ruled me. I found myself eating when not even hungry. I would sometimes eat for no particular reason at all. I'd eat my three meals a day and then some. We can find ourselves eating at breakfast, lunch, or dinner just because "it's time" to eat those particular meals. We don't give a second thought to whether we are hungry or not, we just eat because we are programmed to do so.

I know that for myself, growing up sometimes only having one meal a day and spending a lot of time being hungry, I've fallen into the trap of eating every meal when it was "time" to eat, especially because from past experience I was never quite sure when the next meal would be.

When I started this journey, I thought this would be

the hardest thing to do in the whole entire world. I could not foresee the day when food would no longer be the ruler of me. It recently became very clear to me how much I've changed and have turned the tables on food and how I think about eating, and lucky for me it really did happen easily. It was during my lunch hour and I had errands to do. I lost track of time and didn't have much time to eat (which is usually what I do during lunch). It was then that I realized—I wasn't even hungry. I didn't really feel like eating (that is still a relatively new feeling for me; still trying to get used to it). Thinking about my day ahead; I knew I wouldn't be eating again until 8:30 p.m. The old Lisa would have gone through the McDonalds drive-thru and got a very unhealthy meal, even though she was not hungry, just because it was lunch time and I was "supposed" to eat. The new Lisa stopped and picked up a water and some nuts in the event that she needed a snack to hold her over until dinner. Now I'm not advocating skipping meals, but there are some times when you just are not hungry and you don't want to eat. Why force yourself? Eat when you are hungry, that's not so bad.

Taking control and becoming the ruler sometimes takes a little forethought and preparation. In the past when I was planning trips or being away from home for an entire day, I wouldn't think about meals on the road. I knew there was always going to be a fast food restaurant nearby, I counted on that. With this new way of living I've learned to think ahead and bring along water and healthy snacks, fruit, or granola bars, etc. Believe it or not, it really does help you keep yourself in control.

It's an amazing feeling to realize that food no longer rules my life. I am no longer living to eat, I am officially eating to live. Food is no longer my central focus. The relationship has changed; food is no longer an old friend, it is merely an acquaintance.

COMPETITIVE BY NATURE

I never thought of myself as being competitive. I'd look at friends and family members and watch them get all kinds of silly about who was winning a baseball game, a video game, who had the latest best new toy of the day. I never cared about those kinds of things. Competing about those things did not faze me in the least. Maybe it's because I grew up not having much, so I never expected much. Maybe it's the lack of confidence I always had or feeling like I didn't deserve the best of things or to be a winner. I bought things because I liked them, not because someone else had them. If I was playing a game and I lost, it was really no big deal; after all, it's only a game.

With this new adventure in my life I'm learning, just like everyone "has their price," that everyone is competitive by nature, myself included. The competitive side eventually comes out, you just have to find the thing you are most passionate about and there it is... your competitive side. There are a lot of personality traits that are revealing themselves that I don't recognize. Being competitive is one of them. I will not be shown up on this new journey. I'm determined for many reasons and I would be lying if I said competing was not one of them.

Back in October, I noticed some slight changes with my cousin. Things like she wasn't drinking soda anymore and some of her eating habits had changed. Though it took me a few more months before I began my journey, it was definitely in the back of my head that I did not want her to show me up. I wasn't aware of what prompted her to make her new life choices and I didn't want to ask because she didn't offer, so I figured she had her reasons. Of course I love her to death, we are more like sisters than cousins, so this is a friendly competition, but it raises the stakes for me. It's fun to have someone to compare notes with and push each other by being competitive.

Seems like everywhere I turn these days I have friends and family members doing their own diet and trying to get healthy and lose weight, and while I'm totally supportive of them and excited for them, I can't help but notice it makes me work that much harder to reach my own goals. Especially when it's my brother. I had no idea that my brother was on a diet and had been for a few weeks, and I say, good for him! I think it's fantastic. I want him to be healthy and happy. However, now that I know he's on his own journey, I must stay focused and reach all my goals and succeed and ultimately be a winner. Thinking of myself winning is a bit of a strange statement because in the end, this not a championship sporting event where someone will be declared a winner, but it is part of the game of life where we can all be winners when we reach our goals. And I will do it. I will reach that goal and I will be happy for whoever else is reaching their goals and succeeding right along with me.

I do wonder where this competitive nature comes from. It's quite surprising to me. I'm a person who is easygoing and doesn't get caught up in things like that. I suppose I've found my passion, and nothing is going to get in my way.

It is all in good fun, but don't give me too much credit just yet. I'm not perfect. I have had many a discussion with my cousin about trying to sabotage people's efforts so we can reach the finish line first. The evil plan: Just keep feeding them. Every time they visit, we shall offer up the cake, cookies, pie, and chocolate. Though we don't really do this, it's just something we joke about because it puts a smile on our faces and makes us laugh when we imagine it. I guess being competitive can bring out the dark side as well.

DIETING SOLO

I am sure that those with families who have started any kind of a diet and wanted to try to change the way the whole family eats has heard these words: "Just because you are on a diet doesn't mean that I have to be!"

In the past whenever I started a diet, it was like the whole family was deprived of the things they love even though they have no weight issues.

This time around I'm worrying about myself, though I have stopped buying things like chips and cookies and ice cream on a regular basis, though when they are requested, I will purchase those items. Just because I'm choosing not to eat those things doesn't mean the kids have to give them up completely.

That's part of being a kid, eating cookies and running after the ice cream truck in the summertime.

What I'm trying to teach them is everything in moderation.

INSULTS AND COMPLIMENTS

We all love compliments and I'm no different. I absolutely love it when people notice the weight I've lost, and I look forward to blowing people away when I reach my ultimate goal. I can't wait to see people that I haven't seen in a very long time and watch their reactions when they see me. I love when people tell me that I've inspired them. With each positive comment and compliment I become more confident, I become more inspired, I become more positive, and I work harder at obtaining my goal.

People are funny, and I mean funny in a strange way. While there are so many people that will come forward and offer compliments freely, there are some people who just don't say anything at all. They can clearly see that you are losing weight, but they make no comment even when others are complimenting you right in front of them. I haven't figured that out. Maybe they are smart by not saying anything to you about your weight loss; they won't get themselves in trouble that way. I certainly don't go looking for compliments. I'm proud of myself for what I have accomplished and the compliments are nice and they sure can boost you up, especially when you are having a rough day; however, I'm generally uncomfortable being the center of attention.

It takes a little getting used to. So, it does not bother me when the compliment keepers stay quiet. It's just weird to me how some are so willing to offer it and others keep it to themselves.

Then we have the people who will try to compliment you and fail. And we have the insulters, the ones who will tell you exactly what they think but not realize they are ultimately insulting you.

It's amazing the things people will tell you to your face. I can only imagine what they say behind your back. I've learned that along with the compliments there will be insults, and most of the time the person saying it to you does not even realize that they've said something wrong. I have learned to be the better person and take the insults gracefully. As I've mentioned, I've been a yoyo dieter for many years.

Many years ago, I started a part time job (in addition to my full time job). I had hoped that one benefit of working two jobs is that it would help me eat less, as I'd be just too busy to eat. I again started a diet. I had lost a little bit of weight and had gone out and bought a new outfit. I had to go into my part time job for a training session, and I wore my new outfit. I thought it was very cute: khaki capris, a pretty brown top with little peach flowers, and some new sandals. I felt good and I felt like I looked good. When I arrived at the office all my coworkers commented on how "cute" I looked. It felt good and it was good for my self-esteem. Later that afternoon I was called into the owner's office and was told that she did not approve of my attire. Now let me just say that I was there for training using a vacation day from my full time job. I was not there to work and deal with customers. Let me also say that it is a very small office where I work in the back and don't deal with the public and the dress code is business casual, and other people in the office had worn similar outfits so I thought it was ok.

I sat there and listened, and I use the word listened loosely because at that point I was so angry that she was telling me how unprofessional I looked, I don't think I heard all of her words. I felt my face get hot as it usually does when I reach my boiling point. I didn't let her see how much her words bothered me, but they did. In fact, as I sit here writing this it feels like this was just said to me. I know I shouldn't let these things bother me, but it does. I don't remember what my response to her was. I was as graceful as I could possibly be, I know that because that's what I strive to be. What I did next should come as no surprise to anyone... I ate away the feelings. There went the diet.

Sometimes people try to compliment you and it doesn't come out quite the right way. I was recently approached by a coworker who I'm pretty friendly with. His opening line was, "Don't take this the wrong way." You know you're in trouble when people start a conversation that way. He proceeded to tell me that he could really tell I was losing weight and it showed in my face. Harmless enough right? He continued by saying that the outfit I had on looked good, but when I was heavier, he used to wonder what the heck made me choose certain outfits. To quote him, "What were you thinking?"

I just laughed this off, I knew he meant nothing by it because I know him. But I admit it did get me thinking about what I used to wear vs. what I wear now. I don't think my style has changed very much. I just think that when you are heavy no matter how hard you try, things just don't look quite the way they are supposed to look. I also think that because you are heavy you don't feel good. You have low self-esteem and you carry yourself differently. I feel that with the small amount of weight I've lost I'm walking taller, I'm more confident, and that all comes out. People respond differently to you.

Then we've got the people who have had conversations with me about other fat people. They sit there trying to describe somebody to me and actually say, "They are bigger than you." What am I, the fat meter? I'm the meter to go by, whether someone is bigger or smaller than me. Really? I get it. They just don't know what is coming out of their mouths. Luckily for all of these people I can take things in stride. I know they mean no harm and I've grown a pretty thick skin.

It's pretty bad when you step on the scale and your scale insults you. I turned on my scale the other day, and when I stepped on it instead of my weight I saw O_ld. Either it was telling me I was old or I was an overload. I'm hoping what it really meant is that it needed batteries.

Then we have the people that think everything is all about them. I worked with a crazy woman; she was as eccentric as they come. One day a coworker was complimenting me on my weight loss and this nut job turns around and says, "You know, she's not the only one who has lost weight, I've lost weight too." Really? She then goes to her office and calls me on the intercom and asks, "Can you tell that I've lost weight?" "Ummm, sorry no," was my reply. It's not like she was a big lady to begin with.

I've also noticed that when it comes to compliments it seems like guys are much more open to doling them out. I have a handful of very close girlfriends and they will take notice and let me know what they think, but we are pretty close and want to compliment and empower each other; it's how we've always been. In the outside world, meaning people who are not in my inner circle, when it comes to men vs. women, the men seem to be much more complimentary. Not sure why but it's just something I notice. It's okay to compliment other woman. That's what we should be doing. Lifting each other up.

THE HIGH PRICE
OF BEING FAT

It's expensive to live life in the fat lane. When you travel, if you happen to be the person that has "extra fluff," you will need to buy two airline tickets. That's an expense nobody wants.

When you shop for clothes, fat clothes always cost more. Ever walk into Walmart and see a shirt for $9.99 and in small print it says plus size $13.99?

If you want to eat healthy, well, you can almost kiss that goodbye unless you make a lot of money. Have you been to a grocery store and seen the price of fresh produce? It's very expensive to buy fruits and vegetables, but who has time to have a garden?

Now we can get a burger from a fast food restaurant for ninety-nine cents; cheap enough right? But the high price that we pay is putting that junk into our bodies.

People who do not have a lot of money, like who are on a fixed income, generally don't eat healthy. Take a walk around your local supermarket at the beginning of the month when all the EBT cards have been reloaded. Look in the baskets, you won't find many healthy items in there. I have friends that are on very limited incomes. They need to eat cheap, so they order off the value menus at fast food restaurants. Why? Because good, healthy food is expensive. People will buy what they can afford and what they can afford is loaded with carbs, sodium, and fat. But what can they do? They need to eat so it's a vicious circle.

BRIDESMAIDS

It inevitably happens to every girl out there at least once in their lives. Your phone rings, you answer, it's a dear friend on the other line screaming with excitement. She's engaged and wants you to be one of her bridesmaids. You happily reply, "Of course, I'd be honored."

This is all kinds of fun until you go dress shopping. Not only is it a nightmare to find a dress that is going to look good on you, but you are out shopping with the bride and five other bridesmaids and of course, just your luck, they are all skinny. You are the only overweight person there. So, you can rule out any say in the dress decision making process. It's pure torture watching all these beautiful thin girls try on dresses and looking fabulous in them. As if it's not bad enough to go through this, try having the lady at the dress shop tell you that the chosen dress does not come in a size big enough to fit you, so they need to order extra material. And let's make matters worse... it's said in front of all the skinny girls. Doesn't it make you just want to be the runaway bridesmaid? Again, thoughts of a diet run through your head, but for one reason or another it doesn't happen for you and there you are paying extra money for alterations on a dress you wish would be a size 10.

I have been in a lot of weddings through the years. It would be fun to find all the pictures because there is definitely a progression of weight gain that can be seen in the bridesmaid gowns. Some were normal sizes and as the years progressed the sizes would go up and up until they had to be specially made.

I remember very clearly one of my last friends that got married had asked me to be in her wedding and when we went shopping for the dress, the woman at the store explained how we had to order the extra material. I thought I'd die when I saw my friend's face. She had a look on her face that I couldn't figure out. Was she sorry she asked me to be in the wedding? Was she concerned with the "look" of the wedding? Was she unsure of how the alterations would come out? It was one of the most awful feelings. I felt like I was disappointing my friend. So instead of going on a diet trying to lose as much weight as I could for the wedding, I ate the feelings away. In the end the dresses always looked wonderful, until I put them on. The people who did the alterations did a fabulous job and you couldn't tell that the dress was customized.

The dress isn't the only problem. We also have the problem of pictures. Again, a wedding party of five or six gorgeous skinny girls, and then there's you. Standing next to the skinny girls only makes you look bigger, and makes you more self-conscious of how you look and feel. And wait... how about the person you get matched up with at the wedding, now there's a stressful situation. Either you get paired up with a gorgeous guy and you want to just die because you wonder what he's thinking having to dance with the fat girl, or you get paired up with the only fat guy in the wedding party, now that's a sight.

A TABOO SUBJECT

Let's talk about it... a subject that's not very comfortable for many people. Sex. If you don't want to talk about it... turn the page.

Being heavy affects every aspect of your life, including your sex life. Of course there's the obvious. You go out with your girlfriends and they all look thin and beautiful and sexy. You'll be walking around and some guy will give your girlfriend a look and you think to yourself, that used to be me that the guys would look at, and you want it to be you again. Whether you are looking for someone or not, in a relationship or not, when some random stranger gives you the look it makes you feel good, it boosts your confidence. Being of the heavy nature you know you're not getting that look. Nope, the look, the whistle, and any other comments are going right to your gorgeous sexy friend and we all know where that leads. That leads you right to the carton of ice cream or the jar of peanut butter.

Then there are the things that nobody else sees. The things that go on in the privacy of your bedroom, or the lack thereof, or something in between. No matter what kind of relationship you are in, being fat affects your sex life. When you are thin, you are confident in yourself and the way you look. When you are heavy you don't want anyone looking at you with clothes, why would you want anyone to look at you completely naked?

We all watch TV, we've all been to the movies. We've seen the romantic love scenes that are filmed, the actors are beautiful and they make sex look so fantastic, fun and easy. That's what we all want... but that's not reality. It's clumsy and awkward and makes you aware of your every flaw.

When you are heavy and you have no self-confidence and can barely get through the day without worrying about what people think of you and you feel so crappy about yourself the last thing you want to do is have sex, you'd rather sit down and eat a container of ice cream (and that's how we got here in the first place, curse that ice cream). No matter what your partner looks like they are not going to understand how you feel and it's difficult to explain, so you find yourself going through the motions. It can put a damper on one's relationship.

Now there are the exceptions to every rule and I was talking to an associate about this topic, and she told me that she had a friend whose weight fluctuates and had once said that she has the best sex of her life when she's heavy. I say you go girlfriend! Good for you! For me, it hasn't been that positive and it's because I'm so unhappy about how I look. I have a difficult time believing that someone could love me for who I am and look at me and find beauty and really enjoy being with me on a sexual level. Though my brain tells me that it's possible, my heart won't listen.

EXCUSES, EXCUSES, EXCUSES

I was spending a Saturday evening with some friends and the subject of dieting came up. During the conversation we realized all the excuses people (including myself) use to not start a diet. It's easy to come up with the excuses and hard to make that first step towards a new life.

Have you ever used any of the following:
- Can't start a diet midweek, we'll wait until Monday (Monday comes but the diet does not)
- Too close to the holidays, no sense in starting a diet if I know I'm not going to stick with it with all the festivities
- I'll start in the summer when all the fresh fruits and veggies are out
- Can't start a diet in the winter. It will be easier in the summer when I can go for walks (then it becomes too hot to walk)
- I'm not ready
- I don't have anybody to diet or exercise with
- I need to go shopping for food
- I have that "thing" this weekend; after that

I've used all of these and more. When I was thinking about losing weight this time around, I had a very serious talk with myself and was firm. NO MORE EXCUSES. Christmas was two weeks away and how easy it would have been to say I'll start January 1. I was not going to use that excuse ever again. It takes some kind of crazy person to start a diet right before Christmas and I am that crazy person. I wanted to prove that it could be done.

WHERE HAS ALL THE JUNK FOOD GONE?

Last night I was woken up from a very sound sleep by my son at one thirty in the morning, he was crying because he woke up hungry. I'm a good mother but even the best mothers do not want to be woken up by a nine year old crying because he's hungry. I asked him why he was crying and he said through his tears, "Because I'm hungry and you never buy anything good to eat and when you do everyone eats it."

Let's think about that for a minute. You never buy anything good to eat translates to, you never buy ice cream, Twinkies, brownies, cupcakes, or any other terribly-bad-for-you foods anymore. And when you do buy it on a rare occasion, everyone eats it translates to, because you don't buy that stuff on a regular basis, as soon as it comes in the house it's gone.

I have this to say to you:

1. I'm sorry if I seemed aggravated because you were crying because you were hungry, but it's because we always have food in the house, unlike when I was your age. I was hungry all the time because I did not have the power to get up and just grab a snack (if there were snacks available), I wasn't allowed.

2. There is always something in the house to eat, just because you think there is nothing good because it's not junk food doesn't mean that you can't find something to eat. There were oranges and there were crackers that were easily accessible at one thirty in the morning that should be sufficient.

It's funny how children's views differ from yours or even from reality.

The fact that they think there is nothing good in the house to eat really speaks to me. They don't view fruits and vegetables as something good, they are looking for chips, candy, cake, among other delicious treats.

It also tells me that my shopping habits prior to my new lifestyle must have been very poor if the kids are expecting those treats all the time.

RAISING HEALTHY KIDS

How many times do you see it and wonder? Two or more kids who grow up in the same house and are two completely different beings. It makes you wonder sometimes. Watching both of my kids grow up and viewing their eating habits baffles me. I have a daughter who will live on junk food, ice cream, and fast food, and I have a son who would much rather eat whole meals than the junk (not that he won't eat his share of candy and chips, just that he prefers a meal).

On a typical visit to McDonalds my daughter will order a ten piece chicken McNuggets, a small fries, a McFlurry, and an apple pie. I don't want to even begin to know the caloric intake of that meal. In her defense, she's a dancer and dances about ten hours a week. She can afford the calories. But I worry about her eating habits in the future.

My son is slightly overweight for his build. Nothing to be concerned about at this point, but I can see by his body type that if he doesn't watch what he eats he will have some of his own weight issues.

I did an experiment when the kids were little. I stopped buying junk food and I bought some veggies. I cut them up and put them in a bowl in the fridge. All day long they would open the fridge and pick those veggies out of the bowl and eat them. But like anything else this was work, and as a working mom, I was just too lazy to be doing that all the time.

Because of my own bad eating habits I made a lot of mistakes where food is concerned with the kids. I let them eat too much fast food, I bought too much junk food, I let them drink juice and soda.

I am really hoping that through my journey they will learn the value of good eating habits and see how hard I've struggled to get a grip on my weight issues.

I really wish I had started thinking about all of this earlier and I wish that I had put a little more effort into creating healthier habits for my children.

It takes time and effort to teach children healthy eating habits, but it is time well spent. With the rising obesity rates in this country we owe it to our kids to teach them the value of fruits and vegetables.

THE JOB SEARCH

Two people out of work and looking for a job. They both go for an interview at the same company. One person is thin and beautiful, the other is overweight. Let's just say they are both perfectly qualified for the job. They both interview well. However, who do you think the employer is going to pick? If you chose the thin, beautiful person you'd probably be correct. Now I know this is hard to prove in a court of law but this is how the world works.

I know; I was there. I had left a very good job after fifteen years because of bad managers. I took some time off and when it was time to find a new job, it didn't matter what kind of qualifications I had, I know what they were looking at. They were not looking at my resume, they were not looking at the fact that I could do the job, they were not even looking at me as a person. They were looking at what I looked like, they did not want to hire the fat girl.

I remember one job interview very well. It was for a brand new IMAX theatre opening in a brand new upscale mall. The position was to handle group bookings such as schools and other organizations. It sounded fun. I was interviewed by a petite, pretty young lady. I remember walking into her office and I could tell immediately that she disapproved of my appearance. I knew right away she had already decided I did not have the job. Let's face it, when you are fat, no matter what kind of money you spend on clothes there has been nothing invented yet to hide the fat. We do the best we can with what we have. When I say she disapproved of my appearance I don't mean what I was wearing, but how I looked in what I wore. I shrugged it off and was determined to make this a great interview; after all I needed a job, otherwise I wouldn't have been there.

It turned out to be a great interview, or so I thought. I answered the questions well. We all know when we had a good interview vs. a bad one. I felt this was one of the best I had ever had. Still, the rejection letter came and I knew why.

Now I'm sure there are some of you out there saying, how can you be sure you weren't hired because of your weight? Maybe there was just a more qualified candidate. That is a good point; however, you don't need to be a psychic to know how someone feels. They say that someone can tell if they like you or not in the first thirty seconds they meet you. You can usually go by your gut to know if someone likes you or not. Yes, maybe living in the fat lane for so long went to my head and made me paranoid, but I know in this particular instance I walked into that interview so confident it could be seen. I nailed every question and I saw the look in her eyes that she couldn't wait for it to be over.

It sure would be an interesting experiment to go back to all the places that refused to hire me (once all my weight is gone) and see if they would hire me as the thin girl. Hmm, sounds like a reality show in the making.

DID I REALLY LOOK
LIKE THAT?

Ever have an OH MY GOD Moment? During a summer gathering my photography friend was over. We did a photo shoot to track current progress. After she showed me the pictures she had just taken she kept talking about how she couldn't believe the change. She opened up her phone to show me a picture that she had taken of me about six years ago. All I could say is Oh My God! Did I really look like that? Well of course I did because the camera doesn't lie. Although it has been said that cameras add about ten pounds, so that would be a lie, but still, ten pounds is not all that much.

As I sat there looking at the two photos side by side I could not believe what I was seeing. Yes, there was a drastic physical change, but again, Oh My God! How did I ever let myself get that way? It's easy to see the physical changes as you lose weight, but I'm coming to realize the emotional changes still take time. Losing as much weight as I have has been an exciting journey and I've come a long way, made many changes, but it's still extremely hard for me to look at old photos. I look at those old fat pictures and it's like a knife in my gut. The emotional pain is still there.

The pain of being embarrassed when out in a public place because people are staring at you. The frustration of not being able to find clothes that fit. Remembering how your eyes filled up with tears when you found out that friends and family who are supposed to love you for who you are talk about you behind your back. Finding out that they talk about how they just can't believe how much weight you've gained. Knowing that if they had come to you and told you they thought you should go on a diet it would have caused you just as much embarrassment because you just didn't want to talk about it.

I remember another Oh My God moment. I remember coming home one day and checking my mail. There was a plain white envelope addressed to me. It looked handwritten. I opened it up and there was a newspaper article about some new diet program and a sticky note attached that said, "I thought you could benefit from this." I was so upset thinking who on earth would send this to me? Which one of my family or friends thought it would be okay to send this anonymously? I asked around and of course everyone denied it. I came to find out it was a marketing scam and it didn't come from anyone I knew personally, but now it left me wondering how my name got on the mailing list. Was there a mailing list that was solely for fat people?

A PEBBLE IN MY SHOE

It's funny how the most random things can make you analyze yourself and your life. I headed out for my daily walk and decided to switch my route and enjoy the beautiful scenic bike path. As I went up the street I ended up with a pebble in my shoe. Now most people would stop and empty the pebble out of the shoe immediately. Not me, I said I'll stop when it gets to be too annoying, when I can't stand it anymore. I thought about this and couldn't believe that it was me that was actually making my walk difficult by walking with this silly pebble in my shoe. Why would I do that, why not stop and take it out now?

This got me thinking... I've been doing this my whole life. Doing everything the hard way. Putting up with situations that were annoying and difficult until I just couldn't take it anymore, like the pebble in my shoe.

This is how I got to the point where I had to lose all this weight. I just kept putting up with myself and my bad habits and my lack of interest in exercising and all my emotional baggage until it became the pebble in my shoe that was there for far too long. When I could have stepped back and said you gained five pounds watch what you eat for a week or two.

During this journey I will have to remember when I have a pebble in my shoe, get rid of it right away. It will make life a lot easier.

SOMETIMES LIFE
GETS IN THE WAY

The road to thin is not easy. It takes a lot of work, every hour, every minute, every second of the day. Thinking about every decision you make pertaining to what you eat, when and how you exercise. It can become an obsession. It has to be top of mind awareness. It's when you stop thinking about it you slip back into all your old habits.

Sometimes life gets in the way of all you've accomplished and puts you on a detour. It can be a vacation, it can be having out of town company that stays with you, special projects at work, anything that makes your new routine get out of whack.

Things are going to happen, and you will slip out of your routine. Recently I had my family visiting from Florida for two weeks and my regular routine was interrupted. I cut my walks short so I could spend more time with them. My eating habits were different because Mom cooked a couple of nights and let's face it, there is nothing like your own mom's cooking. I was less strict with myself during this timeframe. I was secretly panicking, thinking that I was going to gain weight. Luckily I maintained it, but now I was beating myself up because if I was a little stricter with myself I would have lost a few pounds.

We have to learn to stop beating ourselves up because life does get in the way. Things come up and it's how you handle it that will make or break your progress. I know that for me the big key to this whole process is getting on that scale every day of my life. When life gets in the way and I don't get on the scale my mind starts playing tricks on me, making me think that I've been so bad. I've been down that road before. Not getting on the scale, thinking I've gained a ton of weight, and letting all my progress go just because I don't want to see the number.

Believe me, it's better to see you've gained one pound and then work extra hard over a couple of days than to wait a month and find out you've gained more than expected and become so frustrated that that small amount of weight escalates out of control and you are back where you started.

Life gets in the way when least expected. We all have issues to deal with, some more than others. I have my moments when I think that I can't take anymore. Maybe I spread myself too thin and give too much of myself to others and sometimes I think I'm just going to explode. Not only do I deal with my own problems but I seem to take on everyone else's problems too. I'm not complaining, I choose to be there and be a good friend, but taking on all the extra stressors of life makes me want to eat. In my short lifetime I have dealt with so many problems, some of them my own, others belonging to the people around me. I've had to deal with child abuse, drug abuse, divorces, deaths, miscarriages, and suicides. These are the major issues that make the minor issues, like how to pay your bills and dealing with your children, seem like mild annoyances. It's no wonder that I have spent so many years of my life eating away the stress and the pain that I've felt.

It's bad enough when you have one major issue going on, but it's like eating a potato chip, you just can't seem to have one. There is usually more than one going on and it makes you just want to lose your mind. I know that it makes me want to run to the refrigerator and eat everything in sight.

They say that there is always someone out there with a situation worse than you, but when you are living through your mom having breast cancer, or losing a child when you are five months pregnant, or having a close relative commit suicide with no understanding why, it's hard to imagine there being something worse. You just feel so bad, so helpless; all you want to do is eat.

I know it's hard but we have to accept that sometimes life does get in the way. Put your big girl or big boy pants on and deal with it. Easier said than done I know especially if you've already been on a diet and lost weight; it can be so easy to suffer a setback. This may be the time when you need to call on your person.

TAKING IT TO
THE NEXT STEP

Once you get into a routine with this new journey you're always thinking about how to take it to the next step. The more weight you lose, the harder it is to keep going. The first few pounds are easy, as you progress though those pounds take more time to come off. I went out for my nightly walk and was using a few brain cells to think about this and thought about what my next step would be. Obviously, every day I make different food choices and there is always room for improvement in my choices. My exercise up to this point has been limited to the elliptical machine, walking, and Xbox dance games.

Knowing that I've got to keep my interest up in exercising and need to constantly keep it fresh so that I'm not getting bored, I wondered what my next step would be. I've always secretly admired runners. I see them running around town and just like our postal workers they are out there in the rain, sleet, and snow. I've often wondered why. The weather was always my first excuse not to get outside for even a walk.

As I walked, I decided to try out jogging. I was unsure of this new movement for myself. I'm the most athletically challenged person you will ever meet. I trip and fall all the time. I have no coordination. In school when the "captains" were picking teams for any kind of recreational sport, I was the kid always chosen last. I'll never forget being chosen last and that whoever ended up with me always rolled their eyes. Yep, that's me, Miss Can't-Run, Can't-Catch-a-Ball, Can't-Do-Anything-Athletic. I can barely walk on two feet sometimes; the times that I've tripped and fallen are countless. My cousin and I spend many a night laughing about all the different times I've landed on my ass. That's the good thing though, I can laugh at myself. I learned how to do that a long time ago.

Well, I got news for y'all—that's about to change. I can't promise that I'll never trip and fall and provide the usual entertainment, but I'm committed to trying new exercise routines and things that I've never done before. This big klutz actually got the nerve to try out the jogging thing and guess what... I loved it. I jogged then slowed it to a walk, then back to a jog again. A good start for someone who has never ran or jogged in her entire life.

I cannot tell you how exhilarating an experience it was (and just for the record, I didn't trip or fall once). This was me, out jogging and in public. Someone who doesn't like people to look at her at all, someone so self-conscious about everything she does, actually moving faster than a walk. I'm at the point now where I don't care what people think when they look at me. I'm doing great things for myself. Last year at this time I probably would have passed out if I tried to jog.

The only thing I can compare it to is a person being paralyzed and being told that they will never be able to walk again. They spend years giving everything they have just to prove the doctors wrong and one day they actually get up out of the wheelchair and walk. That's the exhilaration I felt.

To some, this transition from walking to jogging may not seem like a very big deal. But to me it is. It is showing me that through this weight loss process, I've gone from being out of breath when walking up a flight of stairs to actually wanting to exercise and be healthy. There are people out there who weigh more than I ever did that can understand where I'm coming from. These are the small triumphs that need to be celebrated. These are the small triumphs that I used to celebrate by going out for an ice cream sundae. Now I celebrate by writing about it. The first thing I did as I jogged my way into the house was hop on the computer and updated my Facebook status: just in from a jog. How awesome that sounded. I'm glad I posted because a few of my friends told me about an app called Couch 2 5K. It's an eight week training session, just as it says, from sitting on the couch to getting you ready for a 5K. It's like having a personal trainer in the palm of your hands. Thank you Michelle and Elizabeth for telling me about this. I immediately downloaded this app.

This is such an exciting step that I can finally see myself doing things like walking or running in a 5K race, rollerblading, and maybe someday even skiing. These activities always felt unobtainable to me. They are activities that I always put into that basket of only for the beautiful people. It does make me stop and wonder if my falling down problem has something to do with being overweight as I don't seem to fall that often anymore. I will just have to find another way to entertain the masses.

I DON'T NEED
YOU ANYMORE

One of the nicest things that anyone has said to me during my journey is that ever since I started this process I have been glowing. That statement has been confirmed by a few others who told me they could see my happiness shining through and everything about me was different from the inside out. Let's face it, not every day is going to be a good day and that glow is going to hide on you once in a while. Those bad days are the days that we all need to watch out for.

I had a particularly bad day, what caused it is not important, it's how I felt and how I handled it that is important. Whatever the root of the problem was, it was something that made me feel so terrible. I hadn't been that upset in a very long time. I don't cry often (unless you count crying at commercials, or movies, or watching my daughter dance) but for the most part everyday life doesn't make me cry. There is that rare occurrence when something will hurt my feeling so much I have to run into the bathroom and cry. This was one of those days. Of all places it happened at work. There I was in the bathroom crying and trying to compose myself and it was just about lunch time. This is a dangerous combination.

I needed to run to the local market to pick up a few things I needed for that evening. I walked into the store with my carriage and I could literally hear things calling to me. Delicious things, like whoopie pies, and cookies, and cakes, and cupcakes and pudding and the list goes on and on. They were calling to me because they knew in the past when I was this upset I would not think twice about picking some delicious, fattening sweet treat (and sometimes more than one) to drown my sorrows, to make me feel better.

The wonderful thing about this particular day is that I looked at each and every one of these items and said I don't need you anymore. I've worked too hard, come too far, and tomorrow will be a better day. I don't need to drown my sorrows in chocolate or ice cream or anything else. I held my head up and kept on walking. I grabbed what I needed and went back to work.

I must say I was so proud of myself. It was at that moment that I realized how far I've come. I made it through the day without binging, and the next morning I woke up and I felt so much better and it didn't take eating to do it.

EVERYTHING OLD
IS NEW AGAIN

For someone who hates shopping I've come to the realization that I have an awful lot of clothes. I have drawers full of clothes that are so stuffed it's hard to close them, then there are all the clothes in my closet. The funny thing about these clothes is that many of them are years and years old. There are only a few items that are relatively new. I would buy clothes, wear them a short time, and as I gained weight they didn't fit. I never got rid of them; I just stuffed them in the drawer, probably with the hopes that someday I would wear them again. Someday is here.

As the pounds melt away (and still not liking the whole shopping thing) I find myself wondering, what to wear? I started digging through my old clothes, which are practically new because I didn't get to wear them very often. What a thrill it is to put on a shirt that didn't fit me last summer to have it look really good, and to have it actually show off the weight that I've lost.

It's even amusing when someone comes up to me and asks, "Is that new?" What, this old thing? I'm very glad that I did keep these clothes. It gives me more options, it's saving me a ton of money, and it's saving me the frustration of shopping. I know that in due time that shopping frustration will disappear and shopping will become my new sport. But for now I'm still not at that place.

I was asked recently by one of my coworkers, "How many tops do you own?" I don't think I've worn the same thing twice in a few weeks. That was pretty cool.

Now pants and shorts on the other hand are problematic still. I'm definitely frustrated trying to find new pants and shorts that fit correctly. I'm in the in-between stage for sizes. I tried on my shorts from last summer and they are all way, way too big. A good problem to have, but it's difficult to replace them. A belt is definitely in order. Summer is too short a season to be spending money on a new shorts wardrobe. I've decided to belt the shorts and deal with it in the hopes that once fall hits I will find some decent pants, and next summer will no longer have this in-between issue.

Last week, I met up with a few friends and one of them looked at me and said, "Your pants are too big." Now, I have to say I have never heard that before. I've always had the issue where I would have to stuff myself into pants. Never in my life have I had the "too big" problem. It was definitely fun to hear and it's not the worst problem in the world to have.

WHEN DOES THE DIET END AND REGULAR LIFE BEGIN?

It doesn't matter how much weight you have to lose, whether it's five pounds or one hundred pounds, and it doesn't matter what you call the means to lose that weight. We seem to have an incredible need to put labels and titles on everything so we'll call it a new path, a new journey, watching what you eat, or the most common of all titles: a diet.

We start this diet with a goal in mind. The intention is always once that goal is reached, you don't have to diet anymore. Most of the time we never reach that goal, and we abandon the diet due to boredom or lack of willpower. But what happens when you finally find that you are successful? What happens when this diet consumes your mind and you are always thinking about it, thinking about your choices, good and bad, thinking about exercising, upset when you can't exercise, getting on that scale and watching the numbers go down—Finally!

Does the diet end when you reach your goal? My answer is no. That is one of the reasons why I personally don't refer to it as a diet. It can't possibly end, you can't ever go back to your old eating habits and maintain your success. It has to be a lifestyle, a choice that you make. It has to be a daily effort for the rest of your life. Whatever new lifestyle routine you've chosen, you have to stick with it forever. This is why I'm against any kind of "diet" that makes you drink shakes or use pre-packaged food. To me it's unrealistic, sure that will help you to lose weight, but what is going to happen when you go back to eating "regular" food? You will gain the weight back. The path that I've chosen: simple portion control and exercise. Yes, it is a slow road to my goal, but I'm learning to have control of what I eat and how often. I'm learning that if I have a big lunch, I need to have a small dinner. Will I abandon the diet once I reach my goal? No. It has taken me too long to find my success. I like the results too much to eat the way I used to.

Long ago, in one of my first times participating in the Weight Watchers program, they said nothing tastes as good as thin feels. I finally understand what that means. We all have our favorite foods, but I have finally reached the point where there is no food in the world that would be worth me going overboard on it and gaining the weight back. So, in the end, my answer to the question of when does the diet end and regular life begins is this: The diet actually becomes part of your regular life. Somewhere along the way you will actually forget that you are dieting. It may start off a bit difficult and maybe somewhat torturous, but you will adapt. You will be happier and healthier for it.

SCALE OBSESSION

They say that when you're trying to lose weight, you should weigh yourself once a week. Same day, same time, wearing the same outfit. That's what they say.

Take someone like me who has an addictive personality (it's true, otherwise I wouldn't be in the position of having to lose weight) and a bit of O.C.D. and you can throw the once a week weigh in out the window.

Now, everybody is different but for me, I need to weigh myself every day. This is part of my success. It's when I stop stepping on the scale that I lose track of my progress. Stepping on the scale is the first thing I think of when I wake up each morning. I will get out of bed, go to the bathroom, take everything off—even if it's just a T-shirt I don't care, all clothes must be off, no clothes, no shoes. I step on the scale and here's where the O.C.D. comes in, I have to weigh myself three times in a row to make sure it's accurate. A little crazy I know, but if you haven't picked up on that by now...

I have become so obsessed with the numbers on the scale that I insist on taking the scale with me on vacation this year. It was suggested to me that perhaps they have a scale in the fitness center at the hotel. Well, perhaps they do, but it's not my scale. I need to have the scale that I use every day.

Every once in a while, there will be a day where my routine is interrupted and I slip up and don't get on the scale. Well, I will obsess about that all day long as well. But I won't get on that scale in the evening... I will wait until the next morning, all the while stressing out about what it may say to me since I didn't weigh in the previous morning.

This may all sound a little nutty or maybe even a little "unhealthy" but it works for me. And really, this is the way it has to be for my continued success. I'm okay with letting the scale rule my life. It's worked for me so far. I know from past experiences that once I stop stepping on that scale each day, I will lose my way and I refuse to let that happen again.

SELF DISCOVERY

The day that you wake up and decide that today is the day, you are going to change your life forever by losing weight once and for all, is one of the most amazing days and it will begin such an exciting journey; one that you never imagined.

That day in December started out as another ordinary day for me, I never in my wildest dreams could have imagined where one decision would lead me. That was the day that I decided to finally face this battle head on. I knew deep down that this was it, that I would finally conquer my battle with food, I would change my eating habits. I knew I had that determination and willpower. What I didn't know was how I would grow as a person, the new things I would learn, the new things I would try. I didn't know how much I would discover about myself, or what I would rediscover about myself.

When you gain weight you feel crappy about yourself, there's just no other way to say it, so you stop taking care of yourself. I went years without worrying about putting makeup on or doing my hair. As I started to lose weight and started feeling better about myself I rediscovered beauty products, eye shadow, eyeliner, foundation, lip gloss, hair spray, curling irons... boy did I miss using my curling iron. I even went out and paid twenty dollars for an eye shadow, why? Because I was now treating my successes with other items instead of food, and because I felt good and I wanted to spoil myself and it was fun! I was rediscovering being a girl.

It goes deeper than just getting all dolled up from head to toe. I chose to write this book, which has been so therapeutic, and has led to discoveries about who I really am as a person. I highly recommend that if you are beginning a weight loss journey, keep a journal. Writing is a great way to track your progress and helps keep your goals front and center. You can even start a blog, which is another thing I did. I never thought that deciding to lose weight would bring a book and a blog into my life.

I never thought I would want to exercise. If I travel, it is so important to me that the place I stay at has a fitness center. I used to book hotels for my vacations and say great they have a fitness center, and never ever use them. Now it has become a necessity as this is my new way of life. I've discovered that I want to do more than walk or get on the treadmill. I want to play tennis, I want to rollerblade, I want to be active in every way that I can.

I have discovered that no matter what you have gone through in life, you are the person in control of your own destiny. We all go through bad times, and bad things happen, but we cannot make that our excuse to fail. We have to rise above all of that and find a way to succeed.

I have discovered that I have such a wonderful support team surrounding me. I decided to make this journey public so I could guarantee myself that I would not fail this time and that was one of the best things I could have done. I have found that I have some pretty big cheerleaders rooting for me.

I have learned what a strong person I am, I've overcome so much in my lifetime. I have also discovered new dreams,

dreams of being a published author, becoming a motivational speaker. I have discovered that one path will always lead to another.

I have discovered that I can do anything I put my mind to. It just takes a little self-confidence and motivation.

I have learned that I will stop at nothing to get where I want to go. I have learned that I am someone who is worth more than I thought I was. I have a lot to offer the world and I am willing to share it. I am no longer the scared little girl that everyone used to push around. I will fight for what I want and I won't stop until I get it.

I love making these discoveries and can't wait to see what the next six months are going to bring, the continued weight loss, more self-discovery.

SHADOWS

Just like I've always tried to avoid mirrors, I always hated seeing my shadow. Anything that shows your reflection I avoid. It was just recently that my cousin and I were walking in a parking lot and she said, "Hey, check out your shadow."

I looked down and saw a new, slimmer shadow. It was pretty amazing. That same day I passed a full length mirror in a store and for the first time since I was a teenager, I didn't cringe at the reflection. I didn't love it but I didn't cringe. It's a good start.

WHAT PROGRAM
ARE YOU ON?

When people find out that I'm "dieting" the first thing they ask is, "What are you doing? What program are you on?"

My answer is I'm on the Lisa Diet. Doing my own thing. As I've said before, what works for me is not going to work for someone else. We all have to find our own way. I will tell you what I am doing and you are surely welcome to try my ideas and adapt them into your own program.

Some of the things I'm doing come from advice I'd gotten long ago that always stayed in my head. Some tips that I can offer you that work for me are:

Use a smaller plate. I always used to use my large plate. Now I try as often as I can to use the plate that I used to use for a dessert. Depending on what I'm eating of course. If I'm eating a steak I will use the large plate, it's just easier to cut your meat while other items are on the plate. But the general rule is to use the small plate and only fill it once. When I attended Weight Watchers meetings, the leader would tell us to put food on your plate but never let it touch; that was another portion control method. On the rare occasion that I have ice cream at home, I will use a small coffee cup instead of a bowl, and pasta will go in a small bowl instead of on a large plate.

When choosing the plates and cups that I use, I tend to choose my fancier ones; it's just another Jedi mind trick. It makes me feel like I'm eating something special and I actually enjoy what I'm eating more. Try it, take any food and put it on a paper plate, then put it on a fancier plate. Which one would you go for?

When dining out only eat half. Usually I eat half and give the other half to a friend; this way I'm not bringing it home with me. I used to eat everything on my plate when dining out. The reason I give it to a friend is because I don't want to be tempted to eat the leftovers that night. Dining out is always a challenge because of the extra calories. We all know that if we make the same dish at home that we order out, the home cooked meal is most likely going to be a bit healthier.

I will ask for mashed potatoes instead of French fries.

I only drink water with lemon and sometimes coffee and tea. I've totally cut soda and other sugary drinks out of my life.

When I go to dinner with certain friends we will split a meal instead of ordering our own meals, this is also cost effective.

I cut way back on the pasta. I could eat pasta every day of my life; it's right up there with ice cream. I just don't cook it as much anymore. When ordering it out I'm careful to eat only half.

I don't usually have second helpings. I remember the days of having two or three helpings, now it's rare that I will go back for a second helping.

Chew gum between meals instead of snacking.

Eat what you enjoy. Why waste calories on something you don't really like? I've been at parties and cookouts and have put items on my plate that perhaps weren't my favorites. Don't waste your time or your calories, if you are going to put it in your mouth, enjoy it.

Allow yourself a cheat day. I will usually ease up on a Friday or Saturday, that's usually when the parties and special events are. Be conscious of events during the week; if you are invited to a special event on a Wednesday and you overdo it, don't take your cheat day on the weekend.

Don't deprive yourself, if you want chocolate buy a piece of chocolate. What I usually do is buy a chocolate bar when there is someone around to share it with. I will take a small piece and give it to my friend and instruct them not to give it back to me.

I love to have something sweet after I eat and have often thought that I should just have a bag of Hershey kisses so that way I can have just one. That's a great idea in theory, but I won't buy a bag because I don't trust myself to have just one. The only way that would ever work is if someone held onto that bag for me and really only gave me one after every meal. As much as we change our habits we have to be aware of what our weaknesses are, and sometimes it's just better to not have temptation right under your nose.

Learn your triggers.

Find replacement foods.

REVENGE

They say that revenge is a dish best served cold. I wonder how many calories in that dish? I'm a good person but I'm certainly not above using a bit of revenge for motivation.

How many times have people hurt your feelings? They've said something about your weight or the way you look either to your face or behind your back. They may or may not have meant it but either way it still hurt.

How many broken hearts have you had in your lifetime?

How many times have you wanted to ask that guy or girl out but couldn't bring yourself to do it because you didn't want to risk being rejected because of your weight?

Well my friends, there is nothing better than a little revenge. Whenever you start to slip back into old habits or don't feel like going out for that walk, stop and think about all their faces. All the people that wouldn't give you the time of day when you were larger. Think about their reactions the next time you see them and you are a much thinner person. You are going to stop them in their tracks. They may not even recognize you and it will be you who will have the last laugh.

Sure this may sound a little bitter and not very Christian-like, but c'mon, we've all been there. If it takes the revenge method to keep you moving and keep you motivated then the end result is worth it isn't it?

THE COLD HARD TRUTH

've talked a lot about motivation and triumphs and all the positive things that come with the weight loss journey, but the cold hard truth is it's not always a fun and positive journey. The first six months have been relatively easy for me. The weight dropped at a decent speed, the support system was great, new habits were formed pretty easily, but now that we are surpassing six months the cold hard truth comes into play.

It's hard. It's hard sitting here at the Coffee Depot in Warren, Rhode Island writing and looking up into the bakery case and having delicious pastry staring at you, knowing that not that long ago you would have ordered a decadent seven-layer bar cookie that is second only to those that you make (cut twice the size) and would have eaten with no regrets.

It's hard getting out there and exercising every day, fighting the excuses you could come up with so easily in the past, that are so ready and willing to jump out of your mouth and make you listen. You have to battle those thoughts every day.

It's hard going for that walk, wanting to walk four miles and wondering, if you make the first leg of the journey, how on earth you will make it home.

It's hard walking around town with your friend stopping as they drive by, asking if you want a ride home. It's hard to make the word no come out of your mouth (Note to self: make a T-shirt that says on the front and the back "I'm exercising, I don't need a ride," or maybe "Keep on driving past").

It's hard knowing that right now there is a pint of Haagen-Dazs pineapple coconut ice cream sitting in my freezer and that it's 230 calories for a half a cup and if you break down and eat it you've wasted all that time tonight that you exercised.

It's hard being patient waiting for the results to appear.

It's hard to look in the mirror and still see the fat person that you always see even though people around you seem to notice a difference.

It's hard to juggle diet, exercise, work, handle kids, and run a household.

These are just some of the things that make this journey difficult. I keep telling myself, you will get there, keep working at it, keep doing what you are doing.

Sometimes it's hard to believe that. No matter how great your support system is, and mine is great, this is not their priority. Yes, they will cheer you on, they will listen to you when you ask them to, but you have to be the one to do all this work and believe me, this consumes almost every minute of every day. You can't expect that your cheerleading team is going to be there every minute of every day. They have lives and issues of their own. So remember, even if you have a cheerleader in every corner, they will only come out to cheer for the big noticeable things. They don't want to read your food journal every day, but they will listen to you when you need them to. Just remember this is about you and there will be times you will have to walk the road to thin by yourself, just as you've lived in the fat lane by yourself. Doing this by yourself is hard. Even if you have a friend that is losing weight along with you, that friend has their own path they have to follow. No two journeys are the same. Even though you are traveling this road by yourself, you are not alone. When you really need those cheerleaders they will be there. That is the cold hard truth.

PUTTING THINGS IN PERSPECTIVE

I've lived half my life as a fat person. For half my life this seemed to be my biggest problem (no pun intended). You know what? If I had to have any problems, this is not the worst problem in the world to have. It finally hit me. This is an issue that can and will be solved with some hard work, but this is not the biggest problem in the world. I sit here in the little coffee shop writing and looking around me, and I realize that there are some people out there who would love to be me and only have to lose some weight.

I look at four people who are from a group home sitting there with their nurse enjoying a cup of coffee and they look happy and content, and I think to myself how lucky I am to be able to just get in my car anytime to come here and not have to wait for a ride from my nurse or companion.

I think about parents who have handicapped children, children they may have to push around in a wheelchair because they can't walk, and here I am complaining about exercising.

I think about homeless people who don't know when or where their next meal will come from and I have this weight problem because I eat too much.

I joke about food calling out to me or staring back at me and there are people in this world who can't see or hear.

Thinking about these things really puts this weight issue into perspective. Yes it's hard work, yes there are people out there who really need to lose weight, but compared to so many other problems in this world, this is fixable. So get it together and remember how lucky you are if this is all you have to contend with.

SHOCK, DENIAL, ANGER, AND ACCEPTANCE

The four stages of grief; shock, denial, anger, and acceptance are also the four stages you go through when you step on that scale and find that you have reached your lowest point with the highest number. We all have that number in our head. The number that once we hit it, we will go crazy, and either drives us to eat more out of depression or forces us to do something about it.

I had my number, which shall never be said again, when I stepped onto the scale on that fateful day and saw that I hit a number I swore I would never hit. I was in complete shock. I can't tell you how long I stood on that scale and how many times I re-weighed myself. O.C.D. kicked in overtime.

Then came the denial. No way can that scale be right. It's a liar. There is no way in hell that I weigh that much. Yep, denial all the way. I didn't believe the scale, I didn't believe my clothes that didn't fit, I didn't believe the sizes listed on the tags on my clothes.

Then there is the anger. Anger at myself for getting to this point. What the hell was wrong with me, why couldn't I stop eating? Why couldn't I take care of myself? Why didn't I care? I'd beat myself up all day long. Why didn't anyone say anything to me? Really? You think if someone said something to you that you would have accepted it gracefully? I think you'd say something like this: thanks for telling me I'm fat; just in case you hadn't noticed... you're ugly. Then you'd go home and cry and eat a pint of ice cream.

Finally, acceptance. Accepting yourself for who you are. Accepting that you have a choice to make: you can either live with yourself the way you are at that very moment and maybe continue to gain weight, or you can choose to do something about it. The choice is yours and yours alone.

THE OBSESSION WITH FOOD PHRASES

Not only are we surrounded by food, we are surrounded by food phrases in the way we speak.

- You are what you eat.
- You want have your cake and eat it too.
- The icing on the cake.
- Revenge is a dish best served cold.
- Eat like a bird.
- Drink like a fish.
- The way to a man's heart is through his stomach.
- Taking candy from a baby.
- Sweet as pie.
- Kid in a candy store.

It's just fascinating to me.

JOEY

ohnston Senior High School—thin and possibly pretty. I was popular among the unpopulars. I had a lot of friends but it's safe to say they were the misfits. I was their leader. I have a big heart and hated to see anyone left out or being picked on. I wanted to be accepted into the group of pretty cheerleaders more than anything, but for some reason that just wasn't meant to be. I befriended anyone who needed a friend and this didn't help at all to get me into the elite group of populars. In fact, I remember one evening after my friends went home Dad said to me, "Why don't you ever bring anyone home that is prettier than you?" I looked at him oddly, thinking my friends are pretty. But that's me, seeing the good in all people. I remained in that group of unpretty, unpopular people for the entire ninth grade until I changed schools.

There is one person in particular from my group of misfits that I never will forget: Joey P. Joey was a very large boy, a very nice boy but very large and safe to say not my type. Joey had the sweetest disposition and the kindest heart and he liked me. He would write me poems and lyrics to The Beatles songs and leave them in my locker and I remember wishing that he was thin. I also remember wishing I wasn't so shallow and how I really wanted to like him more than a friend.

I remember the day he asked me out and I told him that I wasn't allowed to date until I was sixteen. Which was the truth. I remember feeling relieved that I had such an easy excuse to use. I liked him as a friend but nothing more. I wasn't attracted to him and I also would have been worried about what people would think and say. It was bad enough that I had already adopted every underdog in school and that got me nowhere on the social ladder.

Why am I telling you this? Because I think about Joey all the time, I think about how I never gave him the time of day and years later I gained so much weight myself. I walked in his shoes. I feel terrible that I was so shallow and judgmental. I always tell my daughter about Joey in the hopes that she will look deeper than the outside appearance of a person. At fifteen years old I wasn't thinking about the inner soul of a person, I wasn't thinking about the sweetness and thoughtfulness of a young man who probably would have treated me like a queen. I was only concerned about the outer appearance and how cute some guy was even when he was a major league jerk to me.

I heard through the grapevine in later years that Joey had lost a lot of weight. I say good for him, and I hope he found a lady who treats him well.

And if this book happens to fall into Joey's hands I hope he will accept an apology from a now much wiser girl who truly appreciates the kindness that he tried to show her all those years ago.

UPSELLING

Everywhere you go people try to upsell you. Thinking back to times when I was less serious about losing weight, the days when I used to eat fast food several times a week, going through the drive-thru ordering whatever number value meal I wanted and an apple pie, I'd always hear, "Would you like two pies for a dollar?" The short answer is no. If I wanted two apple pies I would have asked for two apple pies. I just ordered a sandwich and fries and now you're trying to shove two pies down my throat.

How about going to the movies and asking for a small popcorn? You will get, "Would you like a medium for twenty-five cents more?" Ok, maybe for some people that would be worth it but for those of us who needed to order certain sizes to make sure that we don't overeat, why accost us with the upsizing?

I know this is part of their job, it's all about getting that extra few cents from every customer, but I don't want to be upsold. If I ask for one pie, I want one pie. If I ask for a small popcorn, that's what I want. No more, no less.

PLATE WATCHERS

When I decided that this was it–it was now or never to finally lose this weight—I made a conscious decision to make this a very public journey by telling people, by talking about it on Facebook, and by blogging. I did this because it was it was my way of ensuring my success. I knew people would be watching me and I wanted it that way. I truly believe that doing it would help me be accountable in every way. But, like anything in life there are pros and cons to going public with this journey.

The pros are wonderful. The cheerleading from friends, the encouraging words. Things like having your teenage daughter come home and tell you how amazing you look or when you run into an old friend at the grocery store and hear her tell you how everything about you is different inside and out. These are the things that lift you up and keep you going.

Then there are the cons. The biggest con being what I refer to as the Plate Watchers. The plate watchers are people (people who shall not be named like Harry Potter's Lord Voldemort) who watch everything you put on your plate.

Let me give you an example:

After a birthday celebration (at work) my friend asked me to bring him a piece of cake. I cut a nice big piece of cake and started walking down the hallway. The plate watcher says, "Don't eat that, that's not good for you." Now first of all I have not even discussed my journey with this particular plate watcher. Second of all this cake was not even for me so I would have really liked to throw the cake right in her face.

Now, imagine you've worked super hard over the weekend to reach your goal, top it off with "that time of the month" and you are dying for Chinese food. So you get a plate, a smaller plate than normal. I measured the plate— yes, I did—my normal plate would have been eleven inches in diameter. This plate that I used was nine inches in diameter. I have some rice, some chow mein, one boneless rib, and a fried shrimp. Much less than what I normally would have eaten. I decide to have some more chow mein and I get a look from the plate watcher.

Well Mr. and Mrs. Plate Watcher, you go right ahead and watch my plate all you want. Give me "the look." Tell me I'm eating too much. If you want to irritate me go right ahead and do it. I will tell you this... I am in control. I know what I'm doing. I'm eating like a normal person. I know what I have to do. Thank you for being concerned, I appreciate it but I am being accountable. I get on that scale every morning and I'm doing just fine. I can and will do this. I will not fail. Failure is not part of the vocabulary any longer.

My promise to you and to myself is this: If I feel out of control, if I feel like I'm falling off the wagon... I will ask you to watch my plate, but until then go right ahead and watch. Watch me win!

Oh and by the way, my friend told me to tell you the next time you give me "the look," I should give you "the finger."

T.O.M.

Guys, if you're reading, you may feel free to skip ahead to the next chapter. This may fall into the category of TMI (Too Much Info).

My daughter and her friends refer to the time of the month as TOM. It took me awhile to figure out why but someone must have started it as it's an acronym for time of the month. TOM is different for every single one of us. Some breeze through this monthly curse with no cramps or symptoms at all, and on the opposite end of the scale there are sisters out there that have to take time out of their daily routine because they just can't get out of bed and nothing helps relieve the cramps and/or irritability.

Let me tell you about my personal experience. As a teen I suffered through severe cramps, but my periods were pretty normal as it goes. As I got older and gained weight I noticed that's when the trouble began. I would have periods that would last for two or three weeks. They would be so heavy and I just dreaded this time of the month. It was horrible.

I noticed that every time I had a big weight gain it would get worse. It was so bad that I could just be standing up talking to someone and have a big gush and the next thing I know it would be all over the floor. Talk about embarrassing!

I learned very quickly: when TOM was around, spend most of your time sitting down.

I would go to the doctor and discuss this and they would tell me to lose weight. We even talked about some options, including endometrial ablation, which is a medical procedure where they burn the lining of the uterus and you don't ever have to worry about having TOM again. Sounded too good to be true, but in the end I opted not to have the procedure being the big baby that I am.

As I started losing this weight, I noticed a big difference when TOM arrived. I was absolutely delighted to find that my periods were so light and lasted only three days. At first, I thought it was a fluke, but with every month that passed, I became aware that this was one of the biggest benefits of my weight loss.

NOT PERFECT

Nothing and nobody is perfect. I've dived into this journey the best way I know how. Like everything else in life there are ups and downs and good moments and bad. I've had so many more good moments than bad and I'm proud of myself for that. I'm amazed at the changes and my attitude towards food. I try to consistently have a positive attitude and to keep myself focused on my goal. That being said, I have had a bad day or two. Thankfully not more than that.

The worst day that I can report on was one day when I went home during my lunch break. I had nothing to do that day, no errands to run, nobody around to go to lunch with, so I went home. I opened the fridge to see what was good, unsure of what I wanted. I went to the cupboard, nothing good in there. It was back to the fridge. There was some leftover Chinese so I had that. It wasn't much, just some rice, a spare rib, and a piece of teriyaki. I ate it while watching my favorite soap opera. For some reason it just wasn't satisfying and I needed something sweet. In the freezer was about a half a cup of pina colada ice cream. I thought about and said what the hell. I finished off the ice cream, still not satisfied. I grabbed a small bag of M&M's. As I sat there eating it I knew exactly what I was doing. It was that time of the month and I was using that as an excuse to sneak back into an old eating habit. I was fully aware of what I was doing.

I got up, shut the TV off, and walked out the door. I had to remove myself from the environment before I continued. I thought to myself that I was probably better off going out for lunch because there I have my controlled portions. Instead of beating myself up for not being perfect, I made sure that I exercised a little harder that evening and I just moved on. The old Lisa would have slid right back into those bad eating habits for a few days and started to gain the weight back. I'm sure those plate watchers would have had a field day watching me that day.

Life isn't perfect and we are not perfect. Bad days are going to happen. The important thing is recognizing when you are having a bad day. Knowing makes all the difference. You need to just pick yourself up and move on. Every day is a learning experience. Every day is different. There will be different stressors, different motivators. That is what makes it an exciting journey.

TV VS. REALITY

I don't watch very much television but when I do it's not usually reality TV. I just happened to catch a show called *Extreme Makeover: Weight Loss Edition.* This just happened to catch my eye, especially since I'm going through a similar journey. This particular episode focused on a young lady's weight loss journey for one year starting on her twentieth birthday and ending on her twenty-first. Her original weight was 323 pounds and she lost approximately 166 pounds in one year. Watching this story was so inspiring; at the end of the show she looked amazing. I sat there and cried for her as I was so happy for this person.

One hundred and sixty-six pounds in a year is a lot of weight to lose. I had very mixed feelings as I watched this show. First of all, it was amazing to watch this young lady as she confronted her issues and worked so hard to lose weight. It was a great story and inspirational to anyone who needs to lose weight. It was good TV. But the reality is that not everyone can lose that much weight in a year. As I watched, I couldn't help but think, I've been doing this for six months and have only lost fifty pounds.

I had to stop right there. Only fifty? That's a negative. Fifty is an amazing amount of weight to lose. I had to put it in perspective. There is no way I can sit here and compare my journey to hers. That's when you start getting discouraged. She had a trainer, she had someone helping her. At the end of the show she was given a fifty thousand dollar gift card to Walmart. That is not everybody's reality.

My reality is I work, I have children, I have a limited budget, I have a busy life, and I have to make everything work together. I have other responsibilities to worry about, not just myself even though I am making myself a priority.

There was one line in the show that resonated with me. The trainer said that this young lady had to learn to live a "reasonable lifestyle." That is what we all need to do. To me, living a "reasonable lifestyle" is reality. Reasonable equals living "normally." Reasonable is living and maintaining a lifestyle that incorporates all aspects of your life from work to play and takes your budget into consideration.

So when I see television shows like *The Biggest Loser*, where people take time off from their normal lives and their jobs and spend months doing the program and filming a show I say, good for them. I'm glad they get that opportunity and I'm glad they can do it, but most of us can't do that. So I'm hoping like hell I can put enough effort into this to get to one hundred pounds or close to that within twelve months.

Though you will find similarities no two journeys are exactly the same.

TECHNOLOGY

I never imagined how much technology can help in the diet and lifestyle department.

My new favorite thing is an app that I downloaded on my iPod. It's Couch 2 5K. This app is like having a personal trainer in the palm of your hand. It's a free app (I love free). It's a program that gets you ready to run a 5K in eight weeks. It starts you off walking, then will tell you when to run, and will tell you when to walk again and so on. Each week increasing your running time. It's amazing and something I never thought I would be doing. For those people who do not have an iPod, this is something you can totally do on your own. In fact before I downloaded the app I did start doing it on my own. But I do find that technology can make this process a bit more fun.

Speaking of apps... if you are a Weight Watchers fan, there is a Weight Watchers app that is so easy to use. You can track your points and weight loss and it really helps keep you on track.

There are calorie counter apps, there are weight loss tip apps, and how about a scale that sends all your info to your iPod or iPhone, very cool! It's called the iHealth Scale. I do not own it nor have I tried it, but to me the concept is awesome. You weigh yourself and all the info goes right to your handheld device and you can create graphs and charts on your progress. As cool as it sounds I'm not willing to dish out the cheese to purchase it, especially when I have my faithful trusty scale who I've grown quite attached to.

Xbox and Wii, yes, who would have thought that a video game system can help you lose weight, but there are several fitness based games available. My personal favorite is the Black Eyed Peas Experience. It's a dance game that provides a great workout at every level. There are so many more fitness games; there are a number of dance games as well as Zumba and even a Biggest Loser workout.

There is never ending information on the web. You can go to most restaurant websites and get nutrition information. There is exercise info, there are recipes; with a little planning the computer can be one of your best tools.

There are those who are still without computers in their home so my answer to that is go to your local library. You can use the computer, get exercise books and even exercise DVDs, or for those that still have VCRs, well, check yard sales and eBay and I'm sure you'll be able to find an exercise video to your liking.

For so many years I made excuses why I can't exercise, but there are so many options to help make this journey more fun than work.

Make technology work for you!

CAPTIVATED BY COOKBOOKS

I love books and there is nothing like spending hours at a bookstore or in a library. I love seeing the covers, the titles, and finding that special book that I will spend hours reading. Even more so, I'm captivated by cookbooks.

One afternoon I went to the book store and perused all the different sections and low and behold, I ended up in the cookbook section. I just couldn't help it. They are so colorful, and the photos make everything look delicious. It's like I go into a trance as the beautifully illustrated books filled with cookies, cakes, pies, and more just call to me and drag me over to the cookbook section. I pick each one up and lovingly turn the pages just looking at the beautifully decorated baked goods. Now I should know this all a big trick by now because each time I fall in love with a baking cookbook and I go home and try to match what I see in the book, well, somehow it doesn't look like the picture. Don't get me wrong, I'm a decent cook and a really good baker (yes there is a difference between cooking and baking) but I always get disappointed in the end. I realize that instead of falling for the baked goods books I should be checking out healthy options. What do you think I was drawn to?

I was automatically drawn to the baking cookbooks. I started to think about all the cookbooks I have at home, and I would have to say ninety percent of my cookbook collection is baking cookbooks. I have absolutely no healthy cookbooks. So, I think it's time to invest in a cookbook that provides more healthy options. After all, a person can get tired of eating the same old thing all the time and a book filled with cheesecake recipes isn't going help you lose the weight you want.

BEAUTY & THE BEAST

As a child I had no friends. Growing up in a very strange and abusive environment, the only friends I had were imaginary. I remember one time going outside to play; it was another new neighborhood, and a little girl came over to say hello to me. I was called in the house, no reason was given. The little girl waited for me to come back out for a while. Once she was gone I was told I could go outside and play. I imagine that it was because my birthmother didn't want anyone to know about all of the dark secrets that we had in our house.

I longed to have friends and dreamed of being popular. I remember when I moved in with my dad there was a girl on my bus who befriended me. Her name was Angela, she lived a street over from me. I was so happy that she wanted to be my friend. I remember running home and telling my new mom that I had a friend and Mom gave me the biggest hug. She was so happy for me, she knew what that meant to me.

One of my favorite animated films of all time is Disney's *Beauty and the Beast*. When playing around and being asked if you could be a Disney princess which one would you be, I would always answer Belle from *Beauty and the Beast*. She's pretty, she's smart, she's independent, she likes to read. But it was just recently during my famous girl talks with my BFF (there is nothing in the world like chatting with your BFF about any crazy thing, it's where so much of my inspiration and ideas come from–heck, imagine after years of not having any friends at all, I've got them now) that I discovered I felt a connection to the beast.

All of these years that I have lived life in the fat lane, I have viewed myself to be beastly, ugly, and not someone people want to look at, let alone touch. I spent so many lonely years as a child that when I was older and someone wanted to be my friend I found it so amazing. I remember being in high school; it was the last day of school and we were standing in the gym after class waiting for the bell to ring. One of my classmates, who I just thought was the most beautiful girl I'd ever seen, looked at me and asked for my phone number so she could call me during the summer. I casually gave it to her but inside I was dancing with joy. This beautiful, popular girl wanted to be my friend.

To this day that feeling continues and I know it will never go away. Even as I lose weight and I take care of myself, it is amazing to me that my friends will tell me how important I am to them. My heart melts when they tell me they love me and it melts even more when they come up to me and wrap their arms around me with a hug. All I can think of is a line from my favorite song in Beauty and the Beast; the song is called "Something There" and the line goes like this, "and when we touched she didn't shudder at my paw." You see I feel like the Beast, that nobody wants to be around me, let alone touch me in any way (it all goes back to my childhood I'm sure), but I look around now and I see that I am surrounded by people who want to be my friend, people who want to be in my life, people who really do love and care about me, and I hope that they never tire of me telling them how grateful I am. I appreciate every single one of them because when I'm with them, they make me feel like Belle.

FRAUD

When I started writing this book, I promised to be open and honest. So I want to tell you about a recent conversation.

I was out with friends and we were telling stories and joking around and one of the stories I was telling my friends was how I was at a store one night and I started dare dancing. Now for those of you who don't know what dare dancing is, it's something I've seen on *The Ellen DeGeneres Show* where she has people dance behind unsuspecting people without getting caught. If you don't know by now, I'm the kind of crazy person who will go out in public and do just that.

So, I was telling my friend about being in Target one night and I was dare dancing behind an unsuspecting customer looking at a vacuum. My friend thought it was the funniest thing. I love to make people laugh, (there's that fat comedian syndrome). I continued to tell her about my antics including how I was dare dancing behind a fat person, someone fatter than me because I knew I couldn't be seen. But I also told her how I stopped because I would have felt bad had that person turned around and thought I was making fun of her, and that's completely not what I was doing.

Well, this hit a nerve for someone in my group and that

person got very upset with me and called me a fraud. That person also said that he couldn't believe that I would make fun of other fat people and that I apparently forgot where I came from since I've lost weight.

I could not for the life of me make this person understand that I was not making fun of other fat people. First of all let's call it what it is, it is fat. I would never purposely and intentionally walk up to another person of size (even when I'm thin) and hurt that person's feelings. But as a fat person I feel I have the right to make fat jokes, if you can't laugh at yourself than who can you laugh at. How many comedians out there make fat jokes and people laugh? Not only skinny people laugh at those jokes.

It's like this, you can pick on and joke about and talk about members of your family but if someone outside that circle comes up to you and starts talking about your family, God help them because that is not acceptable. So it's okay for you but not for someone else.

Now back to the fraud part. I could understand this person saying that to me if even at my fattest I never made fat jokes, but I've always found ways to laugh about it. Yes, I've had many hurtful things said to me, I've experienced many painful and embarrassing situations, but I've had many things happen to me that I can laugh at.

We have gotten much too politically correct if you ask me. We are all worried about offending different cultures and races. For the love of God let's just all learn to laugh at ourselves. It is what it is.

I think in the privacy of my own home, or driving in the car among my friends, that I have a right to say what I want to say. However again, let me say that I would never walk up to anyone, a fat person, an ugly person, a handicapped person, a stupid person, or anyone in between and maliciously insult them.

Call me a fraud if you like, I've been called worse!

FABULOUS FIFTY

I started my weight loss journey with a very large goal. I said I wanted to lose one hundred pounds. Between you and me, I was determined but I certainly didn't believe in myself, I didn't think I could do it. It was a nice idea but it still seemed impossible to me.

Nine months traveling the road to thin and I hit the fifty pound mark! I was halfway there. Now I know I can do it. I'm dealing with a much smaller number than when I started.

It's amazing what losing fifty pounds has done for me. I'm wearing smaller sized clothes, I'm taking better care of myself than I ever did before, I won't step out of the house without makeup and curling my hair. Back when I was at my worst I didn't care about how I looked until I ran into people I knew, then I'd beat myself up for not at least trying to make myself presentable.

But it's more than that, it's little things that people take for granted. I dropped something recently and bent down to pick it up and I realized that I can actually bend over to pick something up with ease. I couldn't do this fifty pounds ago. I used to hate playing mini golf because I couldn't bend down to pick up my ball from the hole. I used to make the kids do it for me or if they were not with me, I made sure that I was not the last person to putt. I made a new rule, the last person to putt gathered all the balls; this way I didn't have to bend down.

I can see my feet when I look down. Hello feet, I almost forgot you were there.

I can fit into booths at a restaurant. I don't ask for a table anymore. Just when I finally learned to open my mouth and ask I no longer need to.

I can reach into my drawer and pull out a shirt to wear and find out that it's two sizes too big, that is an awesome feeling.

This one has to be the best one yet... I can wear a bra from Victoria's Secret. I normally don't care about brand names, I'm not materialistic though I like nice things as much as anyone else, but what excites me about being able to wear a bra from Victoria's Secret is it's a store that caters to "perfect bodies." There is no Victoria's Secret plus section. I would not have even known that I could fit into a Victoria's Secret bra if it wasn't for my girlfriend. She had bought two that didn't fit her right and asked if I wanted them. I said sure, I'll try them, and they fit like a glove. It was only then that I looked at the tag and saw that they came from Vicki's. Yes, it's the little things that excite me.

I am also starting to be able to buy clothes from normal stores and not the plus size stores and not the plus size sections. Sometimes this takes a little time and effort, but it is now completely possible. One of my favorite things that I have purchased is a hoodie from Gap. Gap is another store that I have never been able to shop in. I was heading to an outdoor concert in June with a cousin and realized that I had forgotten a jacket. It was a bit chilly so I figured I better have something with me. I was at an outlet mall and wasn't sure where I would find something that would fit me, so I got brave and decided to try Gap as I knew they would definitely have hoodies. The question was, would they have one that fit me? I found an extra large, nervously tried it on, and was elated to see that it did indeed fit. I think I wore that hoodie for three days straight! I was just so excited that I was becoming just like a "normal" sized person and could walk into a "normal" store and find something that fit me.

THEATRE SEATING

I worked for a radio station and we had a ticket give-away for tickets to our local theatre. The ticket winner came in to pick them up; she was a woman of size and she asked me if we had any aisle seats as she has a hard time getting in and out. I never thought of that before. It took me long enough to learn to ask for a table vs. a booth, but when going to the theatre or other venue that has theatre style seating I never thought to ask for an aisle seat. Though sometimes getting an aisle seat is completely out of your control, especially when purchasing tickets through online ticket services. Being uncomfortable in seats at venues can be a deterrent. I can see why someone would much rather stay home and avoid going to places where they would have to be stuffed into a seat.

Seating at these types of places can be very uncomfortable. How do the seat manufacturers decide how many inches wide a seat should be? Who is the decider of what a normal body type is that should fit into a seat?

I have been to the theatre where people of size are sitting side by side and they are both spread out into each other's seats. This is so uncomfortable. I've seen larger people stuffed into a seat taking up space in the next seat over with a skinny person sitting there, and that skinny person is certainly put out.

This is certainly a problem; it's uncomfortable for the person trying to sit in a seat that can't fit and it's uncomfortable for the person that is sitting next to them whether they can fit in their seat or not.

BAD DAY(S)

It doesn't matter what kind of issues we struggle with; it could be it weight issues or some other problem or addiction in our lives, but we all have good days and bad days. That is just the way it works, there is no avoiding them. Thankfully my weight loss journey has been filled with many more good days than bad, but those bad days still occur and I suppose that they always will. It's more important than ever that I practice my newly learned skills and keep moving in a positive direction. It would be so easy to slip back into old habits and sabotage my success and all that I have worked so hard for.

It has taken me many years to grow a thick skin, but every now and then my super sensitive side comes out and someone will say something to me that hurts my feelings. Today was one of those days. What was said to me is minor and irrelevant; it had nothing at all to do with my weight. It was really a misunderstanding, the person saying it meant no harm and certainly had no idea that they upset me. I was also dealing with some major stress issues. Sometimes people will tell me I'm too sensitive and that I shouldn't take things so personally. A lot of the times they are wrong, but in this particular case it really was me being sensitive.

I ended up in the ladies room at work crying and worse than that the old urge of wanting to eat away my sorrow was creeping up on me. I had a serious urge to get that jar of peanut butter and a spoon, or a pint of ice cream, and eat until I just didn't care anymore. At that moment in time I didn't give a crap about all the weight I lost, about all the hard work I put into this new me, and for a moment everything I hated about myself returned.

I had to compose myself and take a good look in the mirror and give myself the ultimate pep talk. I had to remind myself that turning to food was a thing of the past and though it was an old habit that I wanted to immediately turn to, I had the strength to work through the urge. What I did instead was much better for me... I went and got a massage. Getting the massage was certainly much more beneficial for my mind, body, and spirit than an eating binge would have been.

It doesn't matter how much weight I lose or how good I look, I know that I will have to fight off these old habits for the rest of my life. I hope that I always have the strength and mind power to do so.

A DIFFERENT
POINT OF VIEW

I often wonder when I am going to start seeing myself differently. I know I've lost weight, my clothes fit differently, things that used to be tight no longer are. The numbers on the scale have decreased. I've seen a few pictures of myself that I've actually let the public see and in these pictures I can see some changes. I look in the mirror and yet I still feel like the fat girl that I had been for so many years.

I still wonder, when I lose all of this weight what am I going to see in the mirror? Will I still look in the mirror and see the fat girl staring back at me?

Although I still have a difficult time with adjusting to my changing body, I've noticed how other people see and treat me. It's definitely a positive and welcome change. I am no longer being stared at, I can walk into a store a little more comfortably and recently I've noticed that when I'm at a store people who used to call me Ma'am now refer to me as Miss. When this first started happening I was a little confused. I even thought that perhaps it was just a new trend, maybe employers told their staff to refer to ladies as "Miss," as some customers get offended by "Ma'am." When I was standing in line and someone in front of me got ma'amed and I got the "Miss" treatment, well, I had to assume it's because of the weight I lost.

JOURNEY TO THE GYM

It's inevitable that the seasons change and with each change of the season I've had to adjust my routine and change with it. Winter brought the beginning of my exercise routine on my elliptical machine in the basement. Spring and summer were a breath of fresh air, I was able to get out of the house and into a regular routine of walking and eventually began to run, something I never dreamed I'd even want to attempt. That was truly exhilarating and brought such a feeling of accomplishment.

The seasons are about to change again and with autumn almost here and the threat of the winter weather ruining my exercise regimen, I need to be proactive and find a way to stay active. I dreaded the thought of going back to the elliptical. I will jump on it occasionally if I only have time for a twenty minute workout but it's not my first choice of exercise. I just don't like it, mostly because it bores me. I like to have choices, I don't want to be stuck with one method of exercise. I like to use the elliptical as a backup, it's better than not being able to exercise at all. Did I just say that? Wow, imagine that coming from me, someone who just months ago didn't do an ounce of exercise and now it's become part of my life. I actually get upset when I have to miss my exercise. Perhaps the other reason I don't like it is because it's in the back part of my basement. An unfinished, dark dreary place, a little chilly at times and just not aesthetically pleasing. It's no wonder that I couldn't wait to get outside to walk; your surroundings really make an impact on your exercise enjoyment.

Well it is time, time to join the gym. The gym is an expense, it's another bill that I'm not crazy about having but this journey is important to me and, wait for it—here's a news flash—I am important. I am going to complete this journey. I'm going to win the war against fat once and for all and forever. The problem with joining the gym for a lot of people is you dish out a ton of money with the best of intentions of going all the time and utilizing your gym membership to the fullest, and then life gets in the way and you don't get there nearly as often as you want to. I have been guilty of this in the past and it turns out to be such a waste of money. This is one reason I didn't join a gym when I first started this journey. I had to find ways to exercise for free to make sure I was fully committed. Now that I've proved to myself that I am committed to this new lifestyle, I'm going to have to make sure that I utilize my gym membership to the fullest. I am determined to get my money's worth.

Yes there are plenty of exercises that you can do for free. Just because you are committed to a weight loss, new life journey doesn't mean you have to join a gym. It's just a choice that I'm making. I was doing great with my walking routine; at this time I really want to get more serious take classes, use other pieces of equipment that will burn calories, add muscle and tone my body.

I've chosen my gym, it's close to home. They have a lot to offer, including a wide variety of classes. The hours they are open are workable for me and an added bonus is that I know a lot of people that go to this gym. Keeping my journey in the public eye, knowing that I'll be running into friends and neighbors will help me stay accountable to myself.

I'm both nervous and excited about this new workout experience. Nervous because I know I'm getting into the home stretch of this journey and by walking into that gym four times a week I will be surrounded by a wide variety of people. Health fitness nuts, pretty, skinny girls. I'm not there yet, yes I've lost a lot of weight but I have not reached skinny on my meter. I'm excited because I am taking the next step. I am absolutely going to reach my goal; there is no doubt about it. For the first time in my entire life I believe in myself. I am going to do this. I am going to be who I always wanted to be. Yes, on the inside I've always been myself, but the outside hasn't matched my expectations. Maybe along the way I'll meet some new people, some new friends, and maybe also be able to share my story and help others.

I have this vision that I walk into the gym and am surrounded by beautiful people who have been working out for half their lives and here I am, still the fat girl who is clumsy and uncoordinated and hasn't a clue what she is doing. The good news is that I will be getting a session with the personal trainer and they also offer some free nutrition classes. I just have to get past the thinking about the beautiful people and realize that in a few months' time I will be one of those people as well.

I am truly excited about this next level of exercise. I can't wait to see how not only my body will be transformed, but my mind and my attitude and confidence level. I am ready, willing, and able to put in the hard work to make this happen. I can hardly believe that of all people I am going to be a member of a gym.

My best advice when you join a gym is to join one that does not require you to sign a contract. Most gyms will also give a free pass to try their facility. The gym I chose was so awesome—I got a free three day pass even when I said I was definitely joining. When they filled out the expiration date for the gym I noticed that the three day pass actually was for five days. Bonus! When I went in on my fifth day to pay for my membership it was the last week of the month so they just started my billing for the first of the next month, so basically I got another week for free. This to me is exceptional customer service.

If you want to join a gym, shop around. Go talk to the people that work there, choose the one where you feel most at home. When you do that you'll want to spend as much time there as you can. Do not join if you are not committed; don't waste your money like that. It definitely is an investment; it's an investment in yourself.

SOCIAL LONER

love people (well, most of the time when they are not being stupid and aggravating me, stupidity is a major pet peeve of mine). I'm a very social person. I love to go out with family and friends, I love the holidays when my house is full of company, I love to be surrounded by loved ones. It's ironic that someone like that likes to be a loner when I exercise.

I love to go for my walks alone. Don't get me wrong, having company has its perks, but nine times out of ten I want to walk and exercise by myself. It's time for me to chill out and relax. I like to get lost in my music. I get so lost in what I'm doing that there have been times I was walking through my town singing at the top of my lungs (and a singer I'm not) only to have a jogger pass me and I had to chuckle to myself. That poor person who had to listen to me sing! Pretty funny.

I have so many friends (and I love them all) that say hey, when you go for a walk call me. That sounds like a great idea at the time but, think about it. It doesn't matter if it's walking or working out in some other way, everyone has their own routine. It really is a personal matter, just like a computer is a personal thing. Everyone has their own computer set to their liking and what works for them. Same for exercising. We all have different likes and dislikes, we all have different levels of stamina. I can walk faster and further than some and there are others who I can't keep up with.

It's going to be the same thing when I go to the gym. I'm going to take some classes and I will be so scared and nervous because I will feel like I'm the only one there who is a novice. I'm sure there will be so many people there who are so much more coordinated than I am. I just hope that all comes with time and practice and patience.

I'm sure going to a class with a friend could be fun and maybe I'll do that, but for now I've got to go this alone.

TIME TO SAY GOODBYE

I spent the summer wearing shorts that were way too big for me. I belted them up and dealt with it. Still uncomfortable with shopping for new clothing items, I held onto these old clothes like they were a security blanket. I have separation issues and it doesn't just apply to being separated from my family and friends. Apparently I have separation issues with my clothing as well.

I decided this was going to be the last summer I spent with these shorts, forever. I was elated when I tried them on and found that they were all too big and I did try to go to the store to get new ones. The trouble was it was past prime time for purchasing summer clothing items. By the time I got to the store all the good stuff was gone. Anything in my size was gone and I still was not comfortable standing in front of that mirror trying them on, so I got myself a belt. Now that in itself is an accomplishment because I haven't owned a belt in years, it's difficult to find belts in my old size.

As summer turned to fall and I started walking around in my baggy jeans from last year, I had to face the facts. I had to say goodbye to these things. I spent hours going through all my clothes and I was finally able to get rid of them once and for all. They got a good home as they went to my cousin, who was very grateful to receive them.

It was a very strange feeling to be saying goodbye to clothes that I have had for so long, but it was a great feeling of accomplishment. I think part of me held onto them for so long because I still didn't believe in myself, that I was actually losing weight. I mean, what if I gained all of the weight back and then I had to go buy more clothes. Well, guess what? That's the wrong attitude to have. I had to get those clothes out of the house because there is absolutely no going back. I will not keep them hanging around just ready to use that as an excuse. If I kept these oversized clothes by putting them into a big bin in my attic then I felt I would have been giving myself permission to quit my journey at any time. This is not an option.

Yes I will buy new clothes that fit, not because I gained all the weight back, but because I've lost all the weight that I set out to lose and I have every intention of keeping it off.

STAYING ON TRACK

I remember a few months before I got married, my fiancé and I had decided to look into buying a house with the help of his parents. We found a house and I had to go home and tell my own parents that I was buying a house. The next thing I remember is walking into my parents' home announcing that, "I just bought a house," and running up the stairs to my room. From there forward that is how I seem to announce things in my life. Just like that day in December when I woke up and decided to change my life forever. In fact, I don't even think I announced it. I just jumped in and started doing it and made everyone's head spin. What is she up to now?

It's funny how I do that. That's just me. However, I seem to make these decisions and not think them all the way through. I will make a decision and jump right in. So, I must tell you that when I decided to go on a weight loss journey, I had no plan. There was no plan for losing weight, no plan for exercising, no plan for staying on track. I'm making it up as I go along. There was no plan on how to handle stressful situations, though I'm getting better at working through them.

The most obvious way to go about this was to cut out junk and eat smaller portions. Then came the exercise, but what I didn't count on, or think through, was everyday life. Life can come along and sabotage you if you let it. You have to be stronger than that.

While I've been on this journey, I've had my share of moments when life threatened my success. I've dealt with crazy demanding bosses, financial issues, tenants in my rental house that were certifiable and had to be evicted, family members' illnesses (I have had a handful of people in my life over the past year get diagnosed with breast cancer and to me that is way too many). I have friends and family that lean on me for support and as much as I want to be there and help them through everything, it does take a toll on me, though I will never tell them that because I want to be there. I want to help them. It's just that sometimes I get tired and sometimes I just want someone to be there for me.

With each passing day and the stress that these issues brought into my life, there came a challenge. The challenge was to keep doing what I was doing for myself. To keep on keeping with this journey. It would have been so easy to quit, put everyone else first and myself second as I've done in the past.

I'm a very strong person, but sometimes there is only so much you can take. When you have spent the last twenty years turning to food for comfort, that is your first reaction, your first thought. You've got to find a way to stay on track; don't let life get in the way. This is easier said than done, I know.

So how do you stay on track? You've got to learn Jedi mind tricks. My first trick is to turn to exercise; it's amazing how you can exercise your stress away. You've also got to learn to talk to yourself. Go into the bathroom, lock the door, and look at yourself in the mirror. Talk to yourself like you talk to a friend. I know this may sound silly, but I've done it and it really works. Eventually, you will not need to do this anymore. You'll be able to automatically talk yourself down.

I know that there is so much more that life is going to throw my way to try to sabotage me, but I am not going to let it. Every day I wake up and tell myself I can do this, I can complete this journey, I will look great and I will feel great and I will stay on track.

KIDS BEING KIDS

I was standing in the kitchen when my son came up to me and said, "Mom, one of my classmates called you fat." This classmate is the son of a local politician. So being my usual funny self, I told my son to tell his classmate that he just cost his dad a vote in the election.

My serious self was surprised at the fact that when my son told me what his classmate said, I didn't care. Hmmm, sensitive me didn't care? Amazing! I've finally reached that point in my life. Why didn't I care now when in the past that would bother me so much—not the fact that someone called me fat but the fact that it was said to my son?

I'll tell you why I didn't care. First of all, this classmate doesn't know me, so he was just a kid being a kid. Secondly, I know what I've accomplished to this point and I know I will reach my goal. Lastly, I know my son loves me no matter what so it didn't matter. Seems to me that I've found a bit of confidence and self-esteem and you know what? It feels so good.

GETTING STRONGER

When you think of strength you probably think about physical strength. Physical strength can come in handy, especially when you need to beat up your little brother who is physically bigger than you. It's the emotional strength that will get you through the tough times in life. Just when you think that you can't take any more of what life has to throw at you, you find that you've reached the top of that mountain and will be ready to climb the next one.

I am finally able to see how strong I really am. I know that I've handled so much adversity in my life and have come out on top, but to handle the constant change that life brings, even the simplest things make me realize how strong I really am.

I SURVIVED ZUMBA

Zumba, Zumba, Zumba... that's all I've heard about for the past year. Everybody is talking about it. It's fun, it's a great workout, blah, blah, blah.

Being of the anti-exercising club a year ago, I could hardly have cared less about Zumba, but now, I'm going to jump on the Zumba bandwagon.

Zumba is basically an aerobics class inspired by Latin dance and yes, it's fun! It's everything people said it was. Looking for new exciting ways to keep my interest in exercising, I decided to try it. Actually, my very first Zumba class I took reluctantly. I went to the gym to go to a class called Safari. Safari sounded interesting. It was a class based on African dance, so in my head, I'm thinking, ok this could be fun. It was the first class of the session, so my hopes were that I would be in class with many others who had never taken a Safari class before and I wouldn't feel stupid or out of place.

I got to the gym and asked what room the Safari class would be in, and they said, "Sorry, Safari has been canceled today, we are replacing it with Zumba." My inner voice did a little panic. Zumba? *I came here for Safari, oh my god, I can't do Zumba.* I took control of that inner voice and said,

Listen, you're already here give it a try. (I do a lot of talking to myself, have you noticed?)

So I did, the girl who taught it made her announcement of, "Don't worry if you look silly, just keep moving." Here I was, clumsy, uncoordinated me, giving Zumba a try. I stayed in the back of the class; some moves were easier to get than others.

I've recently learned that the trick to most situations is own it. What I mean by own it is just pretend you belong, pretend you know what you are doing. Maybe it's the actress in me but this method of owning it seems to work. For instance there was a time I was in New York City with my kids and one of my daughter's friends, it was a school field trip. Of course one of them had to go to the bathroom at the most inopportune time. A trick I learned long ago is that most hotels have a bathroom in the lobby, but just because there is a bathroom in the lobby doesn't mean that hotels want every tourist to come in and use their facilities, especially in New York (which is why they lock the bathrooms and you need a room key as we found out).

We just happened to be near a hotel that we had stayed at during one of our previous jaunts to the city so I said, "Guys, we are going to walk into the hotel, act like you're staying there, if you get questioned, we are in Room 427." So here we are, the four of us walking in and going right to the bathroom like we knew where it was (well I did know because I really had stayed there before) and we get right to the door to walk in and found out that we needed a room key. The lady at the concierge desk was so nice (yes, that's right, a nice person in NYC), she asked, "Do you need the key?" My reply, "Oh yes, thank you I must have forgotten mine in the room." Now I'm sure the woman wasn't stupid and probably figured out that we weren't staying there, but the point is we owned the situation or at least tried to. So that's just what I did in Zumba.

I stayed in the back of that class, I studied the instructor's moves, I watched the people around me, and in my head I owned that class. Now I know that my feet were a little uncoordinated but I was moving. I had all the arm work down and I left that class sweating. Eventually I will be as good at the Zumba moves as everyone else.

GREAT FEELINGS

There are things that I have discovered over the past few months that make me feel so great. I depend heavily on these feelings to get me over my hurdles, because as we know life brings highs and lows, and it sure seems that the highs do not last nearly as long as the lows.

I've learned that all it takes to make my day great is a few kind words and even a smile can make my day better, so in return I try to tell someone something nice every day. I try to bring positive vibes to people around me and I offer a smile to everyone I can.

Some of the things that just brighten my day may sound silly, but until you go through them you may not understand what I mean.

Ever buy a pair of jeans that are snug and you have to unbutton them to get them off, only to find that one day you can get undressed and can just pull them down without having to unbutton and unzip them? Yes, a very silly thing, but I can tell you that excites me very much.

When I see friends that haven't seen me in a long time and they are shocked and amazed at how I look, well, that just sends me over the moon. It's a way to measure my accomplishment. Of course, after the initial gushing, they keep going on. I start to get a little weirded out because I'm not used to being the center of attention, but it sure means a lot to me.

Leaving the gym drenched in sweat. Yes, it sounds gross, but to me it makes me feel good. When I leave the gym sweating I know I've done exactly what I set out to do. I know it was a good workout.

I can't even describe to you the feeling it gives me when your best friend looks at you and says, "I'm proud of you," or when you overhear your cousin say to your daughter, "Aren't you proud of your mom for all the weight she's lost?"

These may seem like little things, only words, but let me tell you the more you hear them the more uplifted you become.

AN HOUR WITH A TRAINER

With my gym membership I got an hour with a trainer. I set up my appointment and I was of course excited and nervous at the same time. This is a person who has made exercise their life and here I am still overweight, not sure what to expect.

It was a beautiful Sunday afternoon and I could think of things I would like to be doing much more that going to the gym and meeting with the trainer. I made this mess, now I have to pay the price. I walked in with all the confidence I could muster. My trainer quickly put me at ease. We sat and talked, I told him where I've been and where I wanted to go.

He said what we need to do first is get a baseline for measurements. Oh boy... but it was easy. I did have to get on the scale, and that was the first time I got on the scale in front of a person since the last time I had joined Weight Watchers so many years ago. He took my measurements and then we had to take a BMI measurement (Body Mass Index). I've heard of this before and all I could think was, oh my god, this is where I'm told I am morbidly obese, I already know this.

Well, another thing to add to my things that make me feel great list—at this point in time, I was no longer in the very bad range. The chart he showed me had a range that said Normal, High, and Very High. I wanted to jump for joy because I was expecting to be in the Very High category, or in the High at the very least. Nope, I was on the high end of normal. (Thankfully we were just measuring the body and not my crazy personality, that for sure would be at the high end of the very high range).

Holy cow, the weight I had lost up to this point put me into a normal category. Amazing. We then did some warm-up exercises and he showed me how to use the weight machines and put me on a plan.

The whole experience was better than I had imagined.

SURVIVING THE HOLIDAYS

Over halfway to my goal and it's hard to believe that it's coming up on a year when I made a life changing decision. It doesn't matter at what point in the year you decide to change the path you are on, it's inevitable that the holiday season will come back around and slap you in the face. You have to hope that you've learned enough defensive moves that you can block that holiday bitch slap.

October through February has got to be the absolute worst time for people with eating problems. We've got Halloween, Thanksgiving, Christmas, New Years, and Valentines.

The first of the evils is Halloween, bringing candy galore. What have I personally done in the past? Well, I've bought my favorite candy, and being one of the most organized people I know, I've bought that candy well in advance of the actual day that it was needed. There in the house it sat, and I could hear it calling to me. I would break open the bag and take one, and then another and another until I would have to go out to the store and buy more. Halloween would be the day I could have as much candy as I wanted. I would take the kids out trick or treating and come back and raid their candy bags. Now the joke in our house is that the kids are not allowed to come back home until they've gotten a Mounds or Almond Joy. Those are always for me.

My first Halloween of my new life went pretty well, not perfect, but remember, life isn't perfect and this whole journey is about living "normally." I changed several old habits. For starters I did not buy candy until a few days before Halloween so it was not in my house screaming, "Eat me, eat me." Did I buy my favorites like in years past? Not at all, I bought candy I didn't like. It was a mixed bag that contained Jolly Rancher Pops, Kit Kats, Twizzlers, and a few other things that do not float my boat. When the trick-or-treaters knocked on my door I gave them handfuls of candy as I wanted to make sure there was nothing left. I very well know that even though we may not like these kinds of candy, if it's lying around the house and you get into one of those moods—and y'all know what kind of mood I'm talking about, the mood where you will eat anything and everything and then turn around and say that just didn't do the trick—well, it's just better if it's not there at all.

Now the kids came home with a fair amount of candy and as in years past, they did what they were trained to do, they pulled out their coconut candies and gave them to me. Yes! I had two pieces of candy and you know what, that's all I wanted, no more. I could wake up the next morning and be happy knowing that I survived Halloween in a pretty normal fashion. I am fully aware that there are two bags full of candy in my house, but I have learned to tune out the candy that may call out to me.

Thanksgiving can be fairly easy if you keep your awareness up. In our house it's turkey, ham, mashed potatoes, and stuffing, along with various veggies. The stuffing is my weakness. Of course there are desserts, but they are things like apple pie or pumpkin pie. I'm not really a pie person except for that delicious chocolate cream pie that finds its way to my plate.

Christmas Eve to me is the worst of the holidays. We have a huge buffet. Anything from chicken parmesan, eggplant, homemade mac and cheese, a variety of appetizers, desserts. There is enough food to last a week, no kidding. I already know I'm going to give myself permission to eat what I want and then start over again the next day.

LUNCH HOUR

I'm lucky to get a lunch hour, most of my jobs have given me an hour for lunch. I do remember having one job where it was only a half hour and I said to myself, what am I supposed to do with a half hour? I've always been one to get all my errands done during lunch. I've even been known to do my grocery or Christmas shopping during lunch. When I did that I would be on the run and most likely only have time to grab a drive-thru lunch.

The last few years I've been lucky enough to be able to go out with my friends for a leisurely lunch, or I could even go home for lunch if I chose because I live that close to my office. I have noticed that I don't do as well going home for lunch, especially when I don't have a plan.

I've said it before, I love going out to eat. I don't know why exactly, is it because I get served? Is it because I don't have to prepare it? I'm not sure, but what I am sure of is this: whenever I decide to go home for lunch, all I want to do is eat for the whole hour. I turn the TV on and look for something satisfying. Trouble is, it's not often that I'm completely satisfied.

When I go out to lunch, I'm sitting there, chatting, and I get served whatever it is that I've ordered and that's it.

That's my portion done, there is no getting back up to look in the fridge for something else. I get what I get. I'm a great organizer and the best planner ever when it comes to planning a party. When it comes to planning a meal for myself, I'm no good. This is something I've got to work on. Maybe now is the time to dig out all those cookbooks that I hoard in the kitchen. The cookbooks that I buy just because they look nice. Maybe now is the time to really use them and plan, try something new and different and come up with a plan. This sounds good on paper, but it's actually putting it into action that becomes a challenge. Let's see if I can do it, I sure do love a good challenge.

KID IN A CANDY STORE

The expression, "Like a kid in a candy store," expresses excitement and enthusiasm. On the holidays it can become literal. From Halloween to Easter is a very exciting time for those of us who have a sweet tooth. Walk down the seasonal aisle in any grocery store or pharmacy and you will find so many different holiday treats. Some are things you can get year round, just in a variation of colorful wrappers and different shapes. For instance, Reese's peanut butter cups can be found in the shape of a Christmas tree in a red wrapper and egg shaped for Easter. Hershey kisses will be dressed in red and green as well as Easter pastels, and of course Valentines red in between. But then you will find those delectable treats that you wait for all year, like Cadbury eggs, coconut nests, coconut crème eggs, peppermint Andes candies. Even Ghirardelli has a version of peppermint bark.

Being on my journey I was able to resist most of these holiday temptations, but I did indulge in the peppermint Andes candies. I had never seen them before and when I did, I have to admit I got so excited. A new thing to tantalize my taste buds. Unlike the old days, I was able to control myself and not eat the whole package, and I was able to share.

It took me a very long time to get to that point. In the past as soon as they put the Easter candy out it would be feast time. I would buy all the candy for the kids' Easter baskets, put it in my closet, and yes, of course, I would dig in and have to go back to the store and buy more. The kids are older now; the legend of the Easter bunny no longer exists in my house which will make it much easier for me. I will now buy them one chocolate bunny and perhaps a gift card to their favorite store; it's not good for them either. If you hear faint screams of, "Mom, just because you don't eat candy doesn't mean we can't," on Easter morning that sound like a teen and a tween, you can be sure those sounds are coming from my house and two kids who have a serious sweet tooth, on which Mom has pulled the plug.

ROADBLOCK

It happens to the best of us; we hit a roadblock on the journey. It happened to me. Holidays came, life got unbelievably busy and I got stuck. Though the difference this time is my weight loss journey was always on the top of my mind. In the past when I got stuck, I just jumped ship and abandoned my goals. Not this time. Though I remained stuck in one place for a good four months, I never forgot what I achieved and what was yet to be achieved. These things happen. Life happens.

With constant self-analysis and pep talks, I begin the journey again. Breaking through this roadblock, I look at it as phase two. I left myself no choice but to finish this. I made this journey public, I threw away all my old clothes that were too big and with summer on its way, I am going to need to get new clothes. I know that all eyes are watching, and yes, I'm sure there are those out there saying, "She'll never do this," and, "She'll never make it to the finish line." Newsflash: this road block was only a temporary traffic jam. I will reach the end of this road victorious.

Even Walt Disney had many failures before he found success.

Being "stuck" is no fun. The first half of the weight comes off so easily. Then the real hard work starts. There have been a few very difficult months. A typical day for me is to get up at 7:00 a.m., get my son ready for school complete with breakfast, get myself ready for work, drop the boy off at school, be at work at 8:30 a.m., out at 5:00 p.m., head home to pick up my daughter, bring her to dance, do errands, go to the gym, pick up the girl at dance, and head home. It's now 9:30 p.m. By the time I settle down to watch TV we are talking 10:00 p.m. Now I'm up till 1:00 a.m., head to bed and start all over again. That's a simple scenario. Throw in the countless dance competitions, wrestling tournaments, baseball games, and other commitments and it becomes almost impossible to find time for me.

People ask me how I do it. I don't know, I just do, but the most difficult part is taking care of myself, keeping on track with the exercise and the healthy eating.

Most days I have to pick up food on the road.

THE BIG CHEAT
THAT NEVER ENDED

The Langham Hotel, an upscale hotel in the historic city of Boston. Inside this beautiful landmark building you will find Café Flueri and the Saturday afternoon chocolate buffet. Being on a diet, a journey, a new way of life, having lost the weight that I had, I really had no business entering this establishment. It seems as though I let my love of adventure, which also includes my love of food, get in the way.

I had heard about this wonderful, delightful place and I had to see it for myself. All the while saying it was just a one day cheat. I could handle this. Boy, was I mistaken. It was more like the buffet handled me.

Two kinds of hot chocolate, a chocolate fountain for dipping fruits, homemade chips, candy, cakes, cookies, mousse, that's just the beginning. This was an all-you-can-eat, and I did.

It was like a drug addict who had been clean for a year and said, just this once. It doesn't work that way. I continued to eat for the next eight months. I gained every pound back.

All the writing, blogging, working on my book, creating a Facebook page, it was all for nothing. I fell into a bit of a depression. I tried pulling myself out but once you let go, it's hard to get control again.

A NEW INSPIRATION

You never know where you will find inspiration. I was at a dire point, I couldn't stop eating and fell back into the, "I'll start my diet tomorrow," routine. Tomorrow became the next day and on and on. I tried my pep talks to myself, but I just couldn't dig deep enough. I couldn't get motivated, I had no inspiration.

I had not written in a very long time. I didn't want to fail but I just couldn't get restarted. All I wanted to do is sit in my pink chair and watch TV and eat. I didn't know at this point in time that part of the reason I felt like this was because I was sick. All I knew is that I fell off the wagon and I couldn't find the strength that I once had to move forward. Suddenly I found inspiration in a most unlikely place from a person who I never expected.

It's well known among my circle of friends that I'm somewhat of a celebrity stalker. Well, stalker may be too harsh a word but let's call a spade a spade. Truth is, the one thing I desire more than food is to have that acting career. At this point in my life it's not going to happen, I know. I'll be lucky if I can do some local theatre. I made the choice of a different path but it doesn't mean I don't wonder about if I could have made it. I love actors, actresses, singers, songwriters. I admire them so much. They work so hard and they have to give up so much of their privacy because of fans like me. Fans want to know everything about their favorite celebrities.

I appreciated their talent, the work that it takes to go into a production. I'll go to a Broadway show and I always tear up at the end because I've gotten emotionally involved in not only the characters but in the whole experience of the show, knowing that these actors have given everything they have to put on the best performance for an audience. I truly appreciate the arts.

Bret Michaels is front man for the eighties "glam band" Poison. Still touring with Poison, this show was a solo tour. Honestly back in the eighties when Poison hit big I loved their music, but I was not a groupie. I had my hands full with finding out everything I could about Rick Springfield and Def Leppard. Rick and the boys from Def Leppard were my main concern, of course. I had many other singers and groups that I liked ,but as far as having my walls plastered with posters that was reserved for my top two music favorites and of course everyone's favorite: John Stamos, who at the time was Blackie on General Hospital.

I had seen Poison in concert and had a great time, but it wasn't until 2007's premiere of *Rock of Love with Bret Michaels* (VH1's series about Bret trying to find love) that Bret himself caught my eye. I watched the show and for the first time, really got to know (as much as you can know someone via TV) the man that Bret was. What I saw is a "what you see is what you get" kind of guy, a sensitive guy (and that really surprised me). My brother made fun of me for watching the show but there was something about Bret that made me tune in and become a true fan. I could tell he had a gentle soul. I continued to follow his career from Poison to his solo music, to *Rock of Love*, to *Celebrity Apprentice* where he had the winning product for Snapple, a drink called Trop-a-Rocka, which is a diet drink and really does taste good. I learned how he was diagnosed as a child with diabetes, I worried about him when he had a brain aneurysm and heart surgery. I've been to many shows both solo and with Poison (especially when they tour with Def Leppard). I wouldn't miss it. I feel like I have a more mature appreciation for him as an adult than I would have had when I was sixteen.

I never miss an opportunity to go to a concert, I love hearing music of all genres. You really don't have to twist my arm to go many places—a movie, a show, a concert—so when my best friend called me and told me she had free tickets to see Bret Michaels, of course my answer was yes!

May 9 was a night I'll never forget. I left work and met my BFF at the casino where the concert was going to be held. We had some dinner and went to the show. I actually had the opportunity to meet Bret in person that night. While waiting in line (it was a bit of a wait because Bret took his time with everyone, an admirable quality) I had time to think. I was thinking about how much this man had been through with his health and how much he accomplished in his career. I thought about how he had been in and out of the hospital and had to constantly be on watch with his diabetes and yet he doesn't stop. He tours constantly, he seems to always have some kind of reality TV show going, writing music, visiting the troops, he is one of the hardest working guys in show business. I also was thinking about how much weight I had gained and here I was about to get my photo taken with Bret Michaels and I was fat again.

I finally got to Bret and he greeted me with a hug. He was so warm and friendly, I knew I had judged him correctly. He was such a genuine soul. He made me feel like I was the only person in the room. Bret and I had a nice conversation and he looked in my eyes and spoke to me, and for a few moments I was not self-conscious about the way I looked.

I had gone home on such a high and went online to listen to his new song that was debuted at the show. I stumbled across a show he was on recently called *Oprah's Lifeclass*. The premise was that Bret was a life coach telling his story, listening to stories from the audience, relating and offering advice. Some of the things he said, I felt like he was talking right to me. He was so positive. So real. He touches people and he doesn't even know that he is doing it. He can laugh at himself, he takes the time to listen. After watching this show, I sat down and blogged and worked on this book for the first time in a year.

Not only did this experience get me writing again, but thinking of all Bret has been through made me realize I should get myself to a doctor to get healthy again and to get some help with this weight problem. And it's a good thing I did, as I learned I had extremely severe anemia.

I'd love to get another chance to meet Bret and be thinner and get to show him a before and after photo. I'd love to be able to meet my goal weight, publish this book, and bring a copy to Bret.

Thank you Bret for providing me some new inspiration. I really hope I get the chance to bring this book to you.

It just goes to show you that you never know where inspiration will come from.

KICKING ANEMIA'S ASS

spent the winter going to work where I sit all day, going to the next job where I sit for three more hours, and then home for the evening where I sit on my pink Queen Anne chair watching TV and eating myself back to my three hundred pounds. Spring had sprung and I was so depressed, so ashamed. I had worked so hard. I had been so proud of my accomplishment and to throw it all away... again, after saying I would never do that.

At this point I found that I was having a hard time walking up and down the stairs at my house. I would go to work, park my car, and take the very short walk to my office door and I was out of breath. This was not normal. I chastised myself for getting so out of shape again. It was time to ask for help. I hadn't been to the doctor's in four years so I booked myself a physical.

My appointment went great and I spoke very candidly to my doctor about my desire to lose weight immediately. I told her how I did not want any kind of surgery, how I did so well on my own but I may need help now. We spoke about a few different medications and she said before she prescribed me anything she wanted me to have my routine blood work done. Fabulous, no problem.

It took a week for me to get the blood work done as I had to fast for twelve hours, and with my crazy schedule I decided to get it done on the next Saturday that I had off. As planned, I went, gave my blood, and went about my day. Went shopping with my daughter, did errands, had lunch, and headed home as I had to meet my cousins as we had a bachelorette party to get started. It was about one o'clock and my phone rang with an unidentified number. I generally do not pick up numbers I do not recognize and this number kept calling. Finally I listened to the message. "Lisa this is Dr. L, you need to call back right away. We've been trying to reach you for an hour. Your blood results have come back very abnormal."

I was scared to death, what did that mean? Did I have cancer? Was I dying? Talk about being freaked out. I got home and made the call. My doctor sounded relieved to finally hear from me and said, "You need to go to the hospital right away." All I heard after that was the voice of Charlie Brown's mother, you know, the *Whaa whaaa whaa* sound. The few words I could make sense of were, "Your hemoglobin is very low... you do not have enough oxygen in your body... may need a transfusion." So asking her to tell me in a way that I can understand (I'm very bad when it comes to understanding medical situations, my mind just does not compute that) she said my hemoglobin was a 6.8 and should be between 12 and 14. The oxygen level was at 21 and should be over 30. Just as I was hanging up the phone, here come my cousins. I had to tell them change of plans and I explained the situation.

We went to the hospital where I spent the next several hours—more blood work, a brief visit from the doctor. The nurse that brought me to a room asked me how I felt about a transfusion and I said, "I'd rather not have one if there are other options for me, but I will talk to the doctor and see what he says, I'll do what is medically necessary." The doctor came in and said he would work up a plan. Before I knew it I was being discharged with orders to take my iron and follow up with my doctor. I felt fine, or so I thought. I did say that I had some shortness of breath but I attributed that to my weight gain.

I got home early evening, time enough to save the bachelorette party; just had to readjust our plans. Monday came and I followed up with my doctor. That week turned out to be a whirlwind; my general practitioner told me to see my gynecologist, have an ultrasound, and see a hematologist. I will admit I was scared to death; this was more serious than I thought.

As I was driving to my ultrasound appointment, belly wanting to bust from drinking all that water, my phone rang with yet another unknown phone number. I decided to answer it. I heard, "Lisa, this is Dr. S, do you realize that your hemoglobin is very low?" I gave a little chuckle. "Yes Doctor, I'm aware. I've been dealing with this for days now." Dr. S wanted to see me right away but I let him know I was on my way to the ultrasound; he did get me in immediately the next day. Turns out I had a fibroid, which caused my heavy menstruation. He put me on a pill with orders to follow up.

The next day I saw the hematologist; this was the scariest appointment of all. Up until now we had no official explanation of why I was so anemic. I saw Dr. R. She was so amazing. She felt that it was between having thalassemia which is due to my Mediterranean heritage and my heavy menstruation as the cause. She gave me an iron prescription with orders to follow up in a few weeks.

One week after taking the iron, I could walk from the car to my office without running out of breath. I felt amazing. All of those months I thought was feeling ok, I really wasn't. I didn't know I wasn't feeling well until I felt better.

Apparently anemia can be a very serious issue if not treated. Because my numbers were so low and I did not have enough oxygen, this could have affected some vital organs. I had found out that had I kept going I was putting myself at risk for a heart attack or stroke.

If there is a lesson to be learned here, it's go to your doctor once a year. Have your physical. Most important, when your doctor tells you something and you don't understand, ask, and keep asking until your questions are answered. I say this because all the times I went to the doctor's and had my blood work done, I was told, "You're a little anemic." This meant nothing to me. I was instructed to take iron. I didn't. Had I asked questions like what is anemia, what would happen if I didn't take iron, maybe I would not have let myself get so bad, maybe I would have had an understanding of what could happen. So no matter what kind of issues you may have, make sure you have a full understanding of what's going on.

Spending six months undoing all the great things that I had accomplished has left me feeling angry, depressed, anxious, and disgusted. I have to do this all over again. I'm realizing that it may be ok to ask for help. Asking for help is what originally brought me to the doctor's office. I do not want surgery, I do not want to go on a fad diet, I do not want to participate in a diet program where you have prepared meals.

THANKS FOR THE HELP

Sometimes when I'm shopping I'm not sure if I am overly sensitive about my size or not. In general I don't like to be bothered when I'm at a store unless I need help. I like to be greeted when I walk into a store and then when I need a sales associate I like to look up and find that there is not one very far away. There is a chain store that sells soap and body lotions that as soon as you walk in they start telling you all the specials even though there is plenty of signage hanging from the ceiling and on the tables. This annoys me to no end. Half the time I end up walking out.

I was at the Rhode Island Comic Con and was browsing the vendors as I was looking at some T-shirts when Mr. T-shirt vendor looks at me and says the shirts come in all sizes. Well, that's real good to know. I immediately put down what I was looking at and left. He may have been trying to be helpful of course, trying to sell a shirt by letting me know they come in all sizes because I may not have been looking for myself, and because I'm of the larger variety he felt the need to let me know I wouldn't be left out if I was shopping for myself. Perhaps the better way to go with this would have been to say to me, "Let me know if you need any help," then if I was interested I would have asked if he had a larger size.

I proceeded to the next vendor which was a jewelry vendor. She had some lovely rings. As I was looking, again, just looking, she blurted out, "The sizes go up in the row." Again, thanks for being helpful but it made me feel like crap, now I'm looking at my hands. I don't think my hands are fat and chunky. If I was buying I would have asked.

I know, these people are trying to sell their wares. I know that this is most likely all in my head, but when you spend half your life living large you are constantly aware of your surroundings, always thinking about your weight and always thinking that this is what others are seeing and thinking about you too.

IN THE END

Between the never-ending cheat and kicking anemia's ass I'm ashamed, sad, disappointed, and every emotion in between that I fell back into all of my old habits. I stopped exercising, I stopped watching what I ate and there is no excuse. I had the most success I ever had and I blew it. It's like when you go bowling and get a strike; you have to make your next turn count. Everything I learned I threw right out the window.

I have spoken with my doctor several times and this past March. My doctor's office brought in a weight loss program. I made an appointment and went. Upon my first meeting the question of surgery came up. I have thought on and off about it. In fact, I had a specific conversation with my coworker last year and said, "I'm going to give myself one year. If I can't do this on my own in one year I may consider surgery." So when I was asked about having the surgery, my response was yes, I had considered it briefly, but my insurance does not cover it. We tried a regimen of weight loss medication and in my first month I lost thirteen pounds, the next three months nothing. I did some investigation and the health insurance that my employer offers does cover weight loss surgery. I decided that when open enrollment is available I will get covered under my employer's plan and I will go for it.

I met with the bariatric surgeon, Dr. B, and it was decided that I was a candidate.

So, after all of this work, after all the changes I made, losing sixty pounds, I gained it all back. I refuse to give up. I can't! I need to lose this weight, I need to end this battle. As much as I didn't want to have surgery in the past, things change and I feel like this is my last resort. The journey is going to continue, it's just going to continue down a different path. I am taking *The Road To Thin...*

THANKS TO:

Thank you to EVERYONE who supported me in my weight loss efforts and with writing this book. You know who you are.

Special acknowledgements to Stillwater River Publications, Dan Bigelow (artwork), Melissa at East Bay Printing, Megan Northup (initial edits, title, and website), and to the Warren and Barrington Libraries where most of this book was written.

Thank you to all who spent your hard-earned money to buy this book and taking the time to read it. Your support is appreciated.

Made in USA - North Chelmsford, MA
1113479_9781952521133
05.21.2020 0910